D1324893

Ouvrage publié avec le concours du Ministè e français de la Culture - Centre National du Livre.

This work is published with support of the french Ministry of Culture - Centre National du Livre.

A HISTORY OF THE MIDDLE EAST FROM ANTIQUITY TO THE PRESENT DAY

Georges Corm

Translated by Hala Khawam

Garnet Publishing

A History of the Middle East
From Antiquity to the Present Day

Published by
Garnet Publishing Limited
8 Southern Court
South Street
Reading
Berkshire
RG1 4QS
UK

www.garnetpublishing.co.uk

ISBN-13: 978-1-85964-220-7

British Library Cataloguing-in-Publication Data
A catalogue record for this book is available from
the British Library

Printed in Lebanon

CONTENTS

Part III

How to Address the Complexity of the Middle East

INTRODUCTION

The Middle East appears as an opaque and perplexing geopolitical entity to the popular Western eye. The geography and history of the region bear the stamp of mythologies and sacred histories, rendering the Middle East a hotbed for quick and easy analogies and ready-made images. Only a handful of experts – mainly archaeologists – are truly familiar with the peoples and civilizations of the Middle East. Indeed, archaeologists have contributed, in no small measure, to revealing the historical significance of the early civilizations of the Mesopotamian Basin. During the previous two centuries, Europe 'took over' the decadent Middle East, recasting its political geography and refashioning its territories. Due to its strategic location at the crossroads of three continents, namely Asia, Europe, and Africa, and to its abundant oil and gas reserves, the Middle East came to be the source of fierce international rivalries. Consequently, immediately after the downfall of European influence, shortly after the brief Cold War interlude, the United States took the relay and rapidly deployed its armies in the region in an attempt to reshape the Middle East according to its own hegemonic ambitions.

Relentless and brutal struggles and rivalries have marked the history of the region; such violence is well reflected in contemporary literature on the Middle East, be it literary, journalistic, or academic. In the 19th century, Europe sought to save the Christian communities of the East from what it regarded as an intolerable 'decline' triggered by Islam's dominion over the region (some of these 19th-century concepts re-emerged in the media due to the tragic conflicts that beset Lebanon, from 1975 to 1990, and then from

2005 onwards). The Nazi genocide against the European Jewish communities in the 20th century shifted Europe's sympathy mainly towards the future of the state of Israel and that of its Jewish citizens. The creation of the Israeli state in 1948 – symbolizing a 'miraculous' return to sacred history in the collective psyche – unleashed vehement passions among the Western countries regarding the Middle East.

Unfortunately, the 21st century did not start under better auspices than the previous two, as it began with the attacks of September 11, 2001 on New York and Washington by the Islamic terrorist nebula, al Qaeda. These assaults led to the invasion of Afghanistan and Iraq by a military coalition under the aegis of the United States. Thus, the famous 'Clash of Civilizations' put forward in 1993 by American political scientist Samuel Huntington yet again became a focal theme in the new century's geopolitical vision: once more, Islam acted as a fantastical foil to European fears and provided the Western world with another pretext for wanting to control the Middle East.

This book offers a 'profane' overview of the Middle East; by 'profane' we mean a perspective that is neither biased nor imprisoned by religion. Our approach does not consider religion to be the sole marker of historical epochs and of their characteristics, as we believe that there are in fact other, no less significant, factors than the advent of religions; such factors include the geographic contexts, the demographic evolution, the emergence of vast linguistic and cultural groups resulting from the numerous invasions that befell the Middle East throughout the long course of its history, as well as the economic aspects, the region's abundance in energy resources, and the development of techniques, modes of transport, etc.

There is no doubt, however, that the region is the birthplace of the world's three monotheistic religions. Those creeds had a strong impact not only on the Middle East, but also on Europe and considerable parts of the immense Asian continent. Yet they merely succeeded at uniting or at federating the region's various peoples over limited periods of time. This was due to the swarming schisms, heresies, and discordant religious interpretations which arose at the very heart of each of those three monotheistic faiths aspiring to universal domination, divisions which became a constant characteristic of the religious and political history itself. Therefore our survey of the Middle East does not adopt an approach that is exclusively hinged upon religious historical markers.

The first section of this book portrays the evolution of the Middle East from prehistoric times until the onset of the European colonial era. It describes the continuities and the discontinuities that have characterized the Middle East's main civilizational centres since Antiquity. Our approach lays emphasis on the region's main geographical and cultural pillars, which are readily identifiable (Anatolia, the high Iranian plateaus, Mesopotamia, and Egypt) and which have housed its chief political structures throughout its millennial history). It also highlights what we refer to as the 'geology of cultures' which have formed in the Middle East, precisely in these regional geographic pillars, and served as centres for eminent historical empires. Above all, this approach aims to identify the sequence of the region's cultures and political regimes, bearing not only religion in mind but also the cultural and linguistic specificities.

Despite the undeniable importance of the Arab conquest of the 7th century, the religion of the conquerors (Islam) did not abolish the pre-Islamic characteristics of the successive Iranian civilizations and the post-Islamic features of the

Turkish conquerors. Similarly, the advent and spread of Christianity, which was born in the East, did not bring about any tangible change to the main Greco-Roman political structures of the region. In this respect, we shall see that certain cultures, such as the Greco-Roman and its Aramaic and Syriac twins, as well as the Egyptian Pharaonic culture, have indeed managed to survive in the persistence of a myriad of Oriental Churches still present to this day.

The second section addresses the evolution of the modern Middle East, from 19th-century European colonialism to the American invasion and occupation of Iraq. It examines the European colonial incursion, and attempts to explain the decadence that beset the Middle East from the 18th century, in striking contrast to the parallel rise of the European nation-states. Furthermore, it depicts three specific models of resistance to modernization and European domination, i.e. the Turkish, Arabic, and Iranian models, which have not failed to interact with one another.

This section also describes the relative success of modern Turkey in building a new, powerful, and well-respected state over the ruins of the Ottoman Empire. This Turkish success contrasts sharply with the failure of the Arab nationalist movement to fulfil the Arabic-speaking peoples' aspirations to political unity; and more so with regard to the precarious and shaky existence of the Arab states that emanated from the dismembering of the Ottoman Empire. Lastly, this success also contrasts with the Iranian convulsions, which have radiated fierce geopolitical tensions within the region and particularly with the United States since the 1979 revolution. This section also tackles the major conflicts and the cyclic wars endured by the peoples of the region: the Arab–Israeli wars, the Iraq–Iran war, and the two major strikes on Iraq (first in 1991, then in 2003 the American invasion), without forgetting the Lebanese conflicts and the Palestinian tragedy.

The third and final section investigates the continuous decline of the civilizations of the Middle East and the many obstacles it faces, in striking contrast with the rest of the world, in its quest for peace and stability. It also examines the validity of conventional wisdom regarding the Middle East. Moreover, this section attempts to explain the reasons why the Middle East, which has been the cradle of the civilization we presently know as the 'Western world', is still prey to severe cleavages and raging conflicts. This approach adopts a broad scope that goes beyond the simple – if not simplistic – rationales that too often abusively employ Islam as the sole identity and historical marker for the Middle Eastern peoples, and which try to use this religion as the unique key to understand the devastating tremors and hostilities that have been tormenting them for the last fifty years.

This book places those conflicts in a much broader context, including the evolution of global geopolitics and the emergence, in the last few decades, of new political and cultural ways of thinking, especially since the crumbling of the USSR and the Soviet Bloc. It also takes into consideration the American military and imperial deployment in the Middle East made possible by the 1991 Iraqi invasion of Kuwait, a small oil-producing emirate, and later the tragic terrorists attacks in Washington and New York in September 2001. Such events have served to bolster the theory about a 'War of Civilizations', according to which the world is currently divided into two different poles: the Euro-Atlantic, i.e. the countries defining themselves as Judaeo-Christian, and the Islamic bloc, i.e. the countries hostile to the Western world.

Therefore, we will conclude this short historical and anthropological guide by underlining the need to reinstate an impartial implementation of international law in the Middle East. This means that all states and governments should abide by the law – not with a double standard defined by the geopolitical interests or ideological preferences of the Western superpowers – but uniformly so and without any exceptions. The severity of the sanctions imposed on peoples whose governments do not appeal to the Western powers, like the Iraqis for instance, contrasts strikingly with the tolerance granted to other states that can hardly be considered democratic, or to those who refuse to observe the most explicit international resolutions and human rights principles. Quite surprisingly though, such infringements are never sanctioned by UN resolutions and this blatant discrimination unavoidably breeds more violence in the region and greater tensions between the West and what is labelled as the Muslim Orient.

In our overview of the history and the cultures of the Middle East, we shall mainly focus on the Near East, on the east of the Mediterranean, and on Iran. The rich history of the Northern African countries will only be mentioned briefly, by evoking the Arab conquest of the Iberian Peninsula in the first section, and the evolution of the Arab Maghrib in the second section dedicated to the modern Middle East. Despite being closely related to the Middle-Eastern Arab or Arabized peoples by history and language, Northern African countries rapidly gained their autonomy, thus shifting from the centre of Arab power established throughout the Umayyad and Abbasid caliphates, following the invasions of the tribes of the Arabian peninsula in the 7th century.

By presenting the Middle East in 'profane mode' and by putting its long history into perspective on the basis of objective criteria, we aim to free the reader from the stereotyped imagery that the media, but also certain scholars and many Western and Middle Eastern policy-makers, exploit to legitimate the intolerable violence that has been battering the region virtually at a constant pace for over two centuries now.

Part I

Arabesques of Geography and History

1

GEOGRAPHIC AND HUMAN DEFINITIONS

An area with undefined boundaries

Arabesques are light ornamental shapes made of intertwined lines designed by the Arabs. From a geographic, human, and historical standpoint, the Middle East bears a resemblance to an arabesque. By and large, it is defined as a great arc stretching from the tip of the Danubian Plain and the foothills of the Balkan chains in Europe round to the Libyan Desert. The region encompasses Turkey, Iran, Syria, Iraq, Jordan, Israel, the Occupied Palestinian Territories, the Arabian peninsula, and Egypt, namely the Eastern Mediterranean and its direct Asian extension. Certain Anglo-Saxon geopolitical definitions of the Middle East incorporate both Pakistan and Afghanistan into the region and sometimes exclude Northern African countries. (This model was predominant after World War II and throughout the Cold War, when Britain and the United States were seeking to build coalitions with the leading countries of the region in order to fight the expansion of communism.)

All through the 19th century and at the beginning of the 20th century, the 'Eastern Question' was a recurrent and highly widespread theme in diplomatic literature and various essays written by reputable writers and novelists who had undertaken the illustrious 'journey to the East', but it was also very popular with numerous political essayists and eminent scholars. The more metaphorical and poetic term 'Levant' was often employed in reference to eastern Mediterranean countries such as Greece, Turkey, Syria,

Lebanon, Egypt, and Palestine (the Holy Places). However, that term largely fell out of common use and was supplanted by the modern – yet scarcely used – 'Near East' due to the rising prevalence of the Middle East concept.[1] Nevertheless, the borders of the region vary depending on authors and institutions. International organizations, such as the World Bank for instance, often employ the very ungainly expression 'Middle East and North Africa' (MENA); this geographic area curiously excludes Turkey, incorporated in Europe, yet includes Iran together with other Arab countries of the Mediterranean perimeter (Libya, Tunisia, Algeria, and Morocco). Thus, in Anglo-Saxon and French literature, the boundaries of the region remain obscure. With the admission of Greece into the European Union, the western frontier of the Middle East now stops supposedly at the Turkish border, even though Turkey is also a candidate state for EU membership. As for the eastern frontier, it is still unclear whether it stops at the Iranian border, or if it actually comprises Afghanistan, perhaps even Pakistan.

Be that as it may, whatever frontiers are taken into account, one cannot but underline that nowadays – since the beginning of the 21st century – the Arab countries embody the centre of gravity of the Middle East region. It is to be noted that in the mainstream Arab political literature, the Arab world is divided into two main parts: the 'Maghrib', i.e. the Western part (the four above-mentioned North African countries, in addition to Mauritania whose official language is also Arabic), as opposed to the 'Mashriq', i.e. the Oriental part, which comprises the states of the Arabian peninsula (Saudi Arabia, Yemen, Kuwait, Bahrain, Qatar,

---

[1] Additional reading on the delimitation of the region and on the different geopolitical conceptions of its content can be found in Georges Corm, *Le Proche-Orient éclaté: 1956–2007* (Paris: Gallimard, 2007), pp. 63–110.

the United Arab Emirates, Oman), as well as the group of countries belonging to the 'Fertile Crescent', i.e. the Syro-Mesopotamian region (Iraq, Syria, Jordan, Palestine, and Lebanon), and Egypt. The Arabic-speaking countries coalesce under the banner of the Arab League, an institution encompassing 22 member states (the above-mentioned countries in addition to the Sudan, Somalia, Djibouti, and the Comoros). Hence, a more consistent and extensive definition of the Middle East should not only include the 22 member states of the Arab League, but also other countries such as Turkey, Iran, even Afghanistan and Pakistan, as well as the states of the Caucasus where the vast majority of the population is of Turkish or Iranian descent and had long been incorporated to Turkish or Iranian political entities, before being conquered by Tsarist Russia.

This book concentrates on the geographic aspect. But under the term 'Middle East' we only include the Arab countries of the Mashriq, together with Turkey and Iran. In 2005, this 7.2 million km² geographic entity embraced over 330 million people. These can be mainly divided into three different ethno-cultural groups: the Turkish or Turanians (roughly 72 million), the Persians or Iranians (around 68 million), and the Arabs (about 177 million). The Middle East also encompasses numerous minorities. These are relatively significant in number and belong to very heterogeneous ethnic and religious groups, such as the Kurdish, the Armenians and other minorities stemming from Christianity and Islam, as well as the Israelis (6.9 million). The latter are themselves made up of groups from different ethnic and cultural origins. The Ashkenazi Jews, predominantly Russian and Polish, were the first to colonize Palestine at the break of the 20th century; they were later followed by Sephardic Jews who came from North African countries and were descended mainly from the Spanish Jews cast out during the Reconquista; and last of all, came the Berber Jews – mainly Moroccans, Tunisians, and Algerians – and others of Yemeni, Iraqi, Egyptian, and even Ethiopian (the Falachas) origin, who emigrated to Israel after its creation in 1948. Israel retains only a small number of Palestinian Arabs who refused to leave the conquered territory in 1948.

Intertwining mountains, deserts, and seas

In order to fully comprehend the peoples of the Middle East, we must first examine the geography and history of the region, rather than its religious anthropology, despite the existence of a rather widespread vision that seeks to reduce the people of the Middle East to their religious affiliations. This demonstrates the difficulty of defining clear-cut geographic borders in this region of the world, linking between three different continents and several seas. Given its scale, its contrasting geographical environments, or even its millennial history, the Middle East stands out as Europe's polar opposite. Indeed, Europe is characterized by its geographic compactness, its climatic homogeneity, and its relatively short history in relation to other world civilizations.

Europe's only undefined frontiers are located on its eastern side. Indeed, the European continent is bounded by the great icy steppes of Siberia to the north, those of central Asia to the centre, and the high plateaus and mountains of Asia Minor to the south. The Atlantic Ocean and the Mediterranean Sea provide it with natural borders both westwards and southwards. Owing to its small surface area, the climate in Europe is chiefly mild and homogeneous with regular rainfalls and equally distributed hydraulic supplies. Europe's mountain ranges and numerous rivers afford an easy separation between its different political entities and peoples. Even during the imperial era (the Roman, the Holy Roman, and the Austro-Hungarian empires), the modest distances and ease of travel within the European territory made it quite easy to control its peoples. Mountains only occupy small portions of the landscape, surrounding vast fertile plains irrigated by several rivers and watercourses. Europe's geographic position facing several nearby seas has given both men and ideas a great freedom of movement.

The Middle East, however, is cast in a different mould. Its boundaries with Asia, Africa, and Europe are extremely – and virtually inexorably – unstable. Indeed, the peoples of that region have been living at a geographic and human junction since remote antiquity. Repeatedly invaded and infiltrated, from deserts, mountains, and seas, by the peoples of all three neighbouring continents, the people of the Middle East have learned to overcome the utmost hostile natural obstacles, particularly the deserts that bound its southern, eastern, and western sides. Hemmed by seas of water and sand, the inhabitants of the Middle East have also learned to navigate both seas and deserts, which demonstrates their undeniable vocation as a geographic crossroads. They have also learned the languages of their conquerors and immersed themselves in their cultures and religions.

In many ways, the Middle East's geographic features explain its history and its cultural characteristics. Indeed, its geographic environments are diversified and sharply contrasted. Seas border the desert across thousands of kilometres in Egypt and Libya (the Mediterranean Sea), and the Arabian peninsula (the Red Sea and the Indian Ocean); waters also bound the mountains in Syria, Lebanon, Turkey (the Mediterranean and Black Seas), Iran (the Caspian Sea), and the south of the Arabian peninsula (the Red Sea and the Indian Ocean); the desert is hemmed in by mountains as in Iran or Yemen; and the fertile plains are bounded by the desert when approaching sea level (Mesopotamia and Egypt), and by mountains at 1,000 to 2,000 metres of altitude (Lebanon and Iran).

Over very short distances, climates, types of habitat, and populations may vary dramatically. Nowhere, however, do natural obstacles isolate the Middle East's geographic environments entirely as – apart from Yemen – the soaring mountain ranges (e.g., in Iran, Turkey, Iraq and Lebanon) are traversed by large faults, affording easy passageway and access to the fertile valleys and the high semi-desert plateaus.

In total, six main mountainous areas can be identified:

- The Pontic Mountains cover the entire northern part of Turkey and dominate the Black Sea littoral and its subtropical climate; to the east, at the border with the ex-USSR, the Pontic range rises to altitudes of 4,000 metres;

- The Taurus Mountains in southern Turkey spread down to the Alawite Mountain in Syria, and as far as the ranges of Mount Lebanon and Anti-Lebanon, bordering the Mediterranean. To the northeast, the Taurus Mountains culminate at a height of 3,734 metres, while reaching 4,168 metres to the east, at the Iraqi border. The Lebanese mountains can reach altitudes of over 3,000 metres at their highest crests;

- The Zagros Mountains in southern Iran run for 1,800 km from the Turkish border to the tip of the Persian Gulf. Elevations there sometimes exceed 4,500 metres;

- The Elburz Ranges in northern Iran form a crescent-shaped arc and border the Caspian Sea. This mountain system is dominated by Mount Damavand (5,678 metres), an extinct volcano, and Mount Alam Kuh (4,840 metres);

- The mountains of the south of the Arabian peninsula rise to 3,760 metres in Yemen. The influence of monsoons is manifest in Yemeni ranges, which receive relatively large amounts of rain. This explains why that area of the peninsula was called 'Happy Arabia' in Antiquity;

- The desert ranges bordering the Red Sea run adjacent to the Egyptian and Saudi coastlines, and extend to the south of the Sinai peninsula, where peaks rise to 2,637 metres. This range reaches the Jordan Rift Valley in Jordan.

This list illustrates the importance of the Middle Eastern mountain systems. When other areas are added to the above list, such as the Anatolian plateaus of Turkey (1,000 to 2,000 metres in altitude), the Iranian plateaus (sometimes rising over 2,000 metres), the high Yemeni plateaus, and the Lebanese Beqaa Valley (at 900 metres in altitude), it becomes evident that the Middle East is largely inhabited by highlanders. In fact, very large numbers of Iranian, Turkish, Kurdish, Armenian, Lebanese and Yemeni people dwell in vast mountainous areas or in high plateaus.

Desert areas are also quite widespread. Sometimes such areas are hemmed by two mountain ranges (in Iran for example), or bordered by mountains on one side and by the sea on the other. The two foremost desert regions are undeniably the one situated in the heart of the Arabian peninsula, namely Al Rub'al-Khali (approximately 1,000,000 km²), and the Libyo-Egyptian Desert (over 2,000,000 km²), which is part of the Great Sahara Desert. More modest in scale are the Negev Desert in Israel, an extension of the Sinai Desert in Egypt, the Syro-Mesopotamian Desert, an extension of the Arabian peninsula, and the Lout Desert situated in the Iranian Province of Khorasan, famous for its utter aridity and its salty cement covering the sand.

The two major fertile plains of the Middle East are the Nile Valley of Egypt and the basin of the Tigris and the Euphrates (chiefly running in Iraq and flowing to Syria where it makes a long detour). The fertile part of the Euphrates does not exceed 100 to 150 km in width. The mouths of both these rivers die out in a vast area of lagoons and swamps of 150 km in length, opposite the Arabo-Persian Gulf lying at the Iranian border. The Euphrates is 2,330 km long (out of which 1,200 km lie in Iraq). It has an average water flow of 837 m^3/s and has its origin in Turkey, just like the Tigris. The latter is only 1,718 km long (out of which 1,419 km are in Iraq). Owing to five tributaries, which all have their sources in Iraq, its average water flow reaches 1,400 m^3/s – but it can attain 13,000 m^3/s in water level rise, against 5,200 m^3 for the Euphrates.

The Nile Valley in Egypt is much narrower than the Mesopotamian Basin – the soil's fertility merely stretches over a few kilometres – but the river divides into nine arms when reaching Cairo, thus forming a delta of 24,000 km^2 in surface and 260 km in length, bordering the Mediterranean Sea. This is the most fertile and densely populated part of the country. The Nile originates in eastern Africa, at the Victoria Lake in Kenya. Before emptying into the sea, it travels over 6,600 km, out of which 3,000 are situated in Egypt, where its average water flow is however considerably diminished (2,800 m^3/s).

Apart from the Nile, the Tigris, and the Euphrates, the Middle East does not contain any other significant rivers.

Melting snow feeds many watercourses, but these are short-lived, as they arise in spring and die out at the break of summer, evaporating with the first waves of heat. Nonetheless, some countries have more significant watercourses: Jordan and Israel (the Jordan River), as well as Lebanon (the Litani). The significance of areas such as the Mesopotamian Basin, the Nile Valley, the Jordan Valley, and the Lebanese Beqaa Plain – the birthplace of the Litani and of the Orontes which flows on to Syria – shows that the Middle East is also a multi-millennial land of agriculture. It is indeed striking to see the agrarian societies on the banks of the Nile or the Euphrates replicate the same gestures as those depicted on 4,000 to 5,000-year-old Pharaonic monuments and Babylonian steles.

Finally there are the coastal regions. Several seas border all sides of the Middle East. From Istanbul in Turkey to Tripoli in Libya, thousands of kilometres of Mediterranean coastline borders Turkey, Syria, Lebanon, Israel, and Egypt. The Red Sea bounds the eastern flank of Egypt and the Sinai peninsula. It separates Africa from Asia and ends with pliers-shaped arms embracing the Sinai: the Suez Gulf and the Aqaba Gulf, whose tip borders the Israeli–Jordanian frontiers. The Arabian peninsula is bounded by the Red Sea opposite the Egyptian coast, by the Indian Ocean across its width, and by the Persian Gulf waters running deep along the Arabian peninsula to the west, parallel with the Red Sea, and by the Iranian plateau to the east; this is the famous oil region of the Middle East, so called because of the high concentration of hydrocarbon reserves across that shoreline, particularly in Iraq, Kuwait, Saudi Arabia, and Iran. Lastly, in the northeast, the Black and Caspian Seas respectively bound Turkey and Iran. Between these two seas lies the Great Caucasus Range that traverses Georgia and prolongs the vast mountainous plateaus of Armenia and Azerbaijan.

Since ancient times, the Middle East has been home to a vast population of sailors, fishermen, and traders, of which the Phoenicians, characterized by their special connection with the sea, are the perfect archetype.

The Middle East's geographic features largely account for its climatology. Indeed, due to the permanent contacts between the mountainous barriers and plateaus, and fluvial basins on the one hand, and between the deserts and seas on the other, the Middle East is a low-depression area with frequent winds. Constantly pushed by air streams blowing through the sands, the desert advances inexorably unless human action is taken to contain its progression. Rainfall in the Middle East is irregular and often extremely brief and violent. Following periods of heavy snowfall, mountain summits are covered with abundant piles of ice; but massive snow melting sometimes produces floods with disastrous consequences in both rural and urban areas. By and large, rainfall is concentrated over a seven-month period, from November to May, and reaches up to 800–900 mm per year around the Mediterranean shoreline, yet scarcely exceeds 300–400 mm in continental areas and hardly ever attains 100 mm in desert zones. Therefore, as soon as those few river-irrigated areas are left behind, agricultural activities become sporadic in semi-arid zones.

The climate is constantly hot and humid on the plains and in the coastal areas, dry and scorching hot in the interiors, and bitterly cold in winter in the mountains and high plateaus. Despite its abundant water supplies generated by snow melting, the Middle East suffers severe water shortages, all the more so as years of drought are generally followed by years with slightly more frequent rainfalls. As a result, the climate tends to be arid to semi-arid outside the large fluvial basins and certain mountainous areas found in Yemen and Lebanon for instance.

2

THE MIDDLE EAST: HEART AND CROSSROADS OF CIVILIZATIONS

An extraordinary cultural wealth

The Middle East has witnessed a long succession of historic empires and monarchies dating back some six thousand years – a kaleidoscope of shifting political regimes and structures. It is the birthplace of the world's three monotheistic religions, Judaism, Christianity, and Islam. The Middle East is also the native land of Greek and Hellenistic civilization and culture – although this fact has largely been forgotten in our current day and age. Be that as it may, Hellenism strongly influenced the Middle Eastern cultures, which, in turn, equally influenced Hellenism in its development. Moreover, the Orient was home to the Roman Empire which had an enduring influence on the region's institutions and architecture, which was prolonged in the long rule of the Byzantine Empire, itself a Greco-Roman synthesis which lasted until the 15th century. This serves to show that many European cultures have their roots in the Middle East, but also to reveal the extraordinary impact of the Greco-Roman culture on the region's foremost civilizations.

Owing to its strategic position at the crossroads of several continents, the Middle East was destined to interact with the neighbouring cultures. Each mutually marked the other indelibly with its own tincture. Indeed, the Middle East has always fostered close relations with the adjacent Asian civilizations, particularly that of India; while its Mediterranean part, Egypt and the countries of the Arab

Maghrib, has also been in contact with and influenced by the African civilizations. Moreover, large parts of the Middle East were also infused with the Turkish and Iranian cultures which spread into the Caucasus and Central Asia. Elsewhere, in terms of language and history, the culture of the Arab Maghrib countries was profoundly influenced by that of the Mashriq countries.

Eventually, the three main civilizations of the region, i.e. the Persian, Turkish, and Arab cultures, all ended up mutually and greatly influencing each other, forming a brilliant synthesis incarnated by the classical Islamic civilization in the first centuries of its existence. Arabic became the language of high cosmopolitical culture. It was greatly influenced, even if only linguistically, by the Aramaean and Syriac cultures to which it succeeded, but also received significant contributions from Persian and Turkish, as well as from Greek, as evidenced by the numerous Greek loanwords found in Arabic. Following a period of decline in favour of Arabic, Persian meanwhile – written in Arabic script, just like Turkish – underwent an extraordinary renaissance, and many great poets, such as Hafiz and Omar Khayyam, men of science, philosophers, and mystics began to express themselves in Persian.

The rise of modern civilizational fanaticisms in the aftermath of the Cold War has unfortunately obliterated the richness of that cultural legacy from both the Oriental and the Occidental consciousness. It overshadowed the memory of the long history of mutual cultural influences that had prevailed not only within the Middle East, but also between the West and the East. Today, this loss of memory is exacerbated by the region's modern geopolitical context of escalating violence and growing divisions which have bred so-called 'Middle Eastern' or 'Islamist' terrorism. This has created yet another crack in East–West relations, with its epicentre in the Mediterranean region, and served to further deepen the fault line between the Western and the Middle Eastern political cultures.

The origin of this fracture is commonly attributed to the advent of Islam in the 7th century – historically the last of the three rival monotheistic religions. However, history shows that this rift appeared as early as the 4th century at the very heart of the Greco-Roman civilization and culture which prevailed at that time. More precisely, it emerged between the Roman Occidental and Oriental Churches and culminated in the 11th-century schism. The term 'Occident', as opposed to 'Orient', was created to mark this separation within the same civilization and the same religion. In the days of the Ancient Greeks, this distinction did not yet exist because, in spite of their cultural and religious differences, neither Asia nor Europe regarded the other as a rival continent since the Greeks had long been present in both Asia Minor and Egypt.[2]

But we cannot understand such complexity without going back even further, to the very origins of human history.

The birth of the city, deities, and writing

Owing to its strategic position as a human and geographic junction, the Middle East was home to the first urban sites, which were founded in the Mesopotamian Basin and the Nile Valley. It also witnessed the advent of religion and writing at the break of the 4th millennium BC, and the subsequent genesis of civilization.

---

[2] This subject is covered in Georges Corm, *Orient–Occident: La fracture imaginaire* (Paris: La Découverte, 2002).

Recent archaeological finds situate the appearance of the first recorded small-scale settlements in human history around the Euphrates basin, around the 10th and 9th millenniums BC. The first urban sites developed in the 7th millennium BC in what is now Syria, Lebanon, and Palestine; these included Ras Shamra north of the Syrian coast, which was most likely founded around 6500 BC, and Buqras on the Euphrates. The advent of the city of Byblos, the future Phoenician centre lying on the Lebanese littoral, dates back to the 6th millennium BC. In Anatolia, the first village sites also emerged around 6000 BC (Çatalhüyük, Konya plain) and around 6500 BC in Iran. Even then, these civilizations had already developed remarkable technical skills: ceramics, pottery, obsidian craftwork, vases, amulets, furnaces, etc.... In Egypt, however, the first human sedentary concentrations emerged between 4500 and 4000 BC.

An advanced civilization arose in Mesopotamia no later than the 4th millennium BC; it achieved a genuine urban revolution that was to epitomize the remarkable Sumerian civilization. The latter represented a real model of 'world-economy' as it engaged in trade with the Indian continent. Cuneiform writing expanded significantly, which gave rise to the Semitic family of languages (Arabic, Aramaic, Hebrew). Furthermore, several urban centres of that era (Eridu, Ur, Uruk, Lagash, and Umma) bear witness to sheer architectural magnificence. Last but not least, the 4th millennium BC also witnessed the consolidation of several Egyptian cities, in particular Heliopolis (Sun City) and Memphis, which became firmly settled around that time.

Cities served as seats of imperial power embodying superior divinities. Many city temples sheltered clergies, which constituted a fundamental administrative structure. Trade grew intensely and was coupled with a series of developments at many other levels. The Sumero-Babylonian civilization established codes of laws, the most famous being the Hammurabi code (c.1792–1750 BC), described as 'one of the most splendid works in universal history'.[3] The Egyptian civilization also achieved several architectural and pictorial wonders which immortalized its great pharaohs and hieroglyphic writing. The Phoenicians were the ones who perfected alphabetical writing: the first written traces appeared at Byblos around 1800 BC and were developed at Ugarit starting from the 14th century BC. The final version of the Phoenician alphabet was set in Byblos in the 10th century BC; it was adopted by the Greeks in the 8th century BC, followed by the Aramaeans, thus laying the foundations for the subsequent advent of Arabic and Hebrew.

As of the 12th century BC, the Greeks developed urbanism considerably in the Middle East. Asia Minor became home to cities such as Ephesus, Tarsus, Miletus, Heraclea, Pergamum, Halicarnassus, Apamea, Seleucia, Laodicea, and Europus; Alexandria was later founded in Egypt. After that, the Romans entered the region and embossed their own architectural stamp upon every Middle Eastern city which came under their rule.

Since the earliest antiquity, the Middle East has had a unique network of cities which grew denser throughout the ages and came to embrace different strata of cultural, linguistic, and religious contributions. Over the past millennia, these cities were repeatedly invaded and shattered by the nomadic and maritime peoples, even by earthquakes, yet they always rose up from their ashes or were rebuilt at neighbouring sites; the Mesopotamian Basin is but one example of such stubborn endurance. However, the Mongol invasions (1220–1258 CE), immediately following the

---

[3] See Paul Petit, *Précis d'histoire ancienne* (Paris: PUF, 1962), p. 25.

Crusades, brought disastrous consequences (to which we shall return) upon this exceptionally dense network of cities, which was undeniably the cultural centre of universal history. At the break of the 16th century, the Ottoman Empire reunited the Middle East and consolidated stability and security in the region, thus giving those cities a respite and the ability to survive. But it was the European archaeological expeditions of the 19th century, which followed the first French scientific missions that accompanied the Bonaparte Expedition to Egypt, that were to truly give new life to the greatest urban sites of the first four millennia BC.

Population complexity

Owing to its location at the centre of routes linking several continents, the Middle East was due to become a land of great human intermingling between peoples of mixed descent, mainly Semitic and Indo-European but also African through the Nile Valley and Nubia. Coined by German Orientalist, A.L. von Schlözer, the term 'Semitic' designates a set of languages forming a branch of the Sumerian language phylum and its cuneiform writing. It is believed that most of the Semitic-speaking populations came from the Arabian peninsula in migratory waves and settled on the banks of the Euphrates and along the Mediterranean coastline stretching from the Sinai to the Taurus ranges, i.e. the region of the Middle East often called the 'Fertile Crescent', as opposed to the desert and semi-desert areas. The foremost offshoots of such populations include the Sumerians, Acadians, Elamites, Assyrians, Phoenicians, Canaanites, Aramaeans, and Amorites.

Throughout its history (covered in the next chapter), the Middle East was invaded by several peoples from the Urals and Central Asia, belonging to the Indo-European phylum. Those invasions led to complex human and civilizational mixtures. First, the Hittites settled in Anatolia and founded a powerful empire which reached its pinnacle in the middle of the 2nd millennium BC; then came the Kassites and the Mitannians who settled in Iran, followed by the Parthians, Medes, and Persians.

Those important migration movements had their centre of gravity in the Iranian and Anatolian plateaus. They sometimes happened peacefully and sometimes through wars and violence. They were followed by a wave of invasions by 'Sea Peoples'. These were the first to populate Greece and Anatolian Asia Minor, which were still sparsely populated at that time. The Sea Peoples included the Achaeans, Dorians, and Philistines (whose name was immortalized in the term Palestine). Ruined by these invasions which immediately followed those of the Hyksos, the countries of the Fertile Crescent and Egypt fell into decline. This allowed the Greeks, Romans, and Persians to exert their influence over the Middle East for many centuries to come.

The peoples of Turanian or Turko-Mongol descent came from the Ural and Altai Mountains and spoke languages close to Finno-Ugric. They did not come into sight in the Middle East until the 10th century CE, after the onset of Islam and the Arab conquest. They dominated Balkan Europe, the Middle East, and North Africa from the 15th century until the beginning of the 20th century. During these five centuries, many armed conflicts pitted them against other military and political entities in Iran and Central Asia, especially under the reign of the Safavid Dynasty, which revived Iranian civilization.

Lastly, the Crusades carried out by European peoples – such as the Germanics, the Normans and many others – in the Eastern part of the Mediterranean from the 11ᵗʰ to the 13ᵗʰ century CE, also left their marks on the region. These are largely visible in certain Lebanese and Syrian families bearing names of European origin, although they subsequently came to be totally Arabized. The region also bears the imprint of the foremost Italian cities that dominated the Mediterranean after the Crusades; Genoa and Venice in particular deeply influenced the architectural style of the Middle Eastern coastal areas.

This brief exposé reveals the complexity of the Middle East's population and more particularly, the impressive length of its history. In our day, it has become possible to datemark and to even reconstitute ten to twelve millennia of history, eight out of which are situated before the advent of Christendom, against barely three millennia in Europe. Such diverse strata of civilizations and populations render the Middle East – now impoverished and partitioned into artificial political entities based on the European nation-state model – a land of obscure complexity. This is why we should examine the major cultural strata which shaped its geology of civilizations, regardless of the preconceptions and the political partitions engendered by colonialism and de-colonialization.

The geology of cultures in the Middle East

The Middle East is a land of great diversity, a mosaic of different ethnic and cultural features which cannot possibly be reduced to a uniform bloc. Nomadic life undeniably marked the region, but the permanence of cities of high civilization despite a largely nomadic and tribal environment shows that urban life is also a millennial feature of the Middle Eastern landscape. The contributions of nomadic life were very heterogeneous, the fruit of two migratory waves from both the south (the first came from Arabia by camel), and the north (the Indo-European peoples followed by the Turanians came from the northeast by horse). Those arriving from the south founded the illustrious Acadian and Sumerian urban civilizations, as well as the remarkable network of Phoenician maritime and trade cities; while those arriving from the north founded the Persian and Greek civilizations, both of which were subsequently influenced by the earlier Sumerian and Assyrian substrata. Nomads and city dwellers fostered complex relations; an interaction described best by Ibn Khaldun, the great Arab historian and sociologist, in respect to classical Islamic civilization.

Thus, the opposition between Semitic and Indo-European (Aryan) peoples is hardly relevant in analyzing the cultural features of the Middle East. This approach was largely popularized in Europe in the 19th century through the works of Ernest Renan and Arthur de Gobineau. However, history shows that the populations of those two linguistic groups intermingled greatly, which proves this dichotomy purely artificial. This interpenetration is further evidenced by the extent of linguistic interplay. Arabic for instance – which is an archetypal Semitic language, comprises many Greek and Persian (Indo-European phylum) loanwords, while Persian and Turkish (up to the 20th century) are written in Arabic script. Such interactions symbolize perfectly the cultural and human intermarriages characterizing the Middle East. Thus, the Aryan/Semitic dichotomy only seems relevant in respect to linguistics: the ancient Hebrews may in reality have been nomads originating from what is known as Indo-European (or Aryan) Asia, but so were the Philistines, the ancient ancestors of present-day Palestinians, who came via the sea...

Yet, European culture has reduced the image of Semites to merely the Jews and the Arabs... It was also direct contact with the ancient Mesopotamian, Assyrian, and Egyptian high civilizations that helped fashion Greek thought and enabled the Greeks to emboss their cultural imprint upon the cultures of the Middle East, from the beginning of the 1st millennium BC until the demise of the Byzantine Empire in 1453.

Such cultural interactions were particularly fruitful in the realm of religion, where the foremost Sumerian and Egyptian theological constructions, the dual concept of good and evil in Persian Mazdaism, and the Greek Platonic school of thought, helped fashion the very structure of Monotheism, i.e. the belief that only one deity exists, according to which God is the sole Legislator, the Regulator of the universe, the Supreme Judge between good and evil. Moreover, the transposition of the Greek notions of citizenship and barbarity into the monotheistic 'believer/unbeliever' dichotomy, along with the biblical notion of 'The Chosen People', and the substrata of the ancient Egyptian, Mesopotamian, and Persian theocracies, helped erect elaborate systems of imperial administration. After Antiquity, those systems were embodied by two major Arab caliphates, namely the Umayyad and the Abbasid, as well as the Byzantine and Ottoman empires.

The nomadic peoples have also greatly influenced the development of arts in several Middle Eastern and Eastern European populations with their music and poetry. Indeed, striking similarities and analogous structures can be found in Greek, Bulgarian, Romanian, Turkish, Armenian, Kurdish, Caucasian, Iranian, and Arabic music. This is also true of Middle Eastern cuisine, although some cities like Esfahan, Aleppo, or Istanbul now outrank the others in culinary refinement and variety.

Be that as it may, the Middle East can be divided into three major cultural and linguistic ensembles, each subsuming its own religious or ethnico-national pluralism: the Turkish, Iranian, and Arabic ensembles, each having broad extensions outside the Middle East.

The *Turkish world* extends to numerous peoples of the Moslem-populated republics of the ex-Soviet Union. Until World War I, many Turks and Turkish-speaking communities could be found in Greece and in the Balkan countries, which underwent a long spell of Ottoman rule. Similarly, many Greeks lived in Turkish coastal cities. However, the emergence of nationalisms propelled by European political ideas disrupted this harmonious blending of populations, typical of the Middle East and the Indian peninsula.

The deportations of populations were inevitably accompanied by their fair share of massacres, the most tragic being the Armenian genocide. At the end of the 19th century and during World War I, the Armenians found themselves trapped by European policies; some 800,000 Armenians died in the course of those brutal events. They were the victims of the cynicism of the European superpowers and of the convulsions of the dying Ottoman Empire. The millennial (over one-thousand-year-old) Armenian lands lying to the east of the Anatolian Plateau and around Lake Van were completely deserted and the Armenians lost their homeland. They were forced into exile; some fled to Soviet Armenia, Lebanon, and Syria, and others migrated to France and the United States where they formed Armenian diasporas. The territory of modern Turkey also contains a number of Arabs, albeit on the path towards Turkicization, who can still be found mainly in Antioch (Antakya) – which remained Syrian until 1939. The largest non-Turkish community, however, is without doubt the Kurdish community (comprising approximately 8 million Kurds), which can be found in eastern Anatolia and along the borders with Iraq and Syria. Even so, Turkey is a relatively homogeneous state with respect to religion, as the Kurds and most of the Arabs still living there are all Sunni Muslims. To the east, however, there subsists an important community of heterodox Muslims, i.e. the Alawites, which currently comprises five to six million followers.

The *Iranian world* is no less complex. It also comprises a wide spectrum of ethnic groups as a result of the Turkicization of the northern part of the country by the Seljuk Turks beginning in the 13th century CE. The Azeris, a people of Turanian descent, have clustered in Iranian Azerbaijan and formed a compact bloc of seven to eight million people. This bloc extends beyond the Iranian frontiers and overlaps the newly independent Republic of Azerbaijan (a former Soviet province). In Khuzestan, in the south of Iran, lives a significant community of Arab peoples, an extension of the southern part of the Iraqi Mesopotamian Basin. The Baloch, an offshoot of Pakistani Baluchistan, inhabit the eastern corner of the country. In addition, Iran comprises a Kurdish community dwelling along the borders with Turkey and Iraq, as well as numerous Turkmen tribes and other small minorities, namely the Armenian and Assyrian Christians. From a religious standpoint, while Shia Islam is the predominant confession even among the Turkish-speaking Azerbaijanians, the remainder of the country's communities (Arabs, Kurds, and Turkmen) belong to Sunni Islam. From a linguistic angle, besides Persian (Farsi) – which is the predominant and official language of Iran – and Turkish, a number of other dialects are spoken by the different nomadic and seminomadic groups. Those dialects comprise many Turkish, Persian, and Arabic loanwords, which demonstrates yet again the intense cultural interplay that characterizes the Middle Eastern ensemble.

The *Arab world* is an emblematic Semitic sphere which can be divided into four areas: Egypt and the Sudan; the countries of the Fertile Crescent (the Mashriq) – Syria, Lebanon, Palestine, Jordan, and Iraq; those of the Arabian peninsula – Saudi Arabia, Yemen, Oman, the United Arab Emirates, Bahrain, and Kuwait; and those of North Africa (the Maghrib) – Libya, Tunisia, Algeria, Morocco, and Mauritania. The Maghrib and the Mashriq have a common history and heritage dating from the Phoenician era. The Arab conquests suppressed Christianity in the Maghrib, but not Judaism. In fact, the Arabs Islamicized most of the region, but failed to achieve total linguistic Arabization. The Berbers for instance managed to retain their language (Amazigh) as well as several other dialects. They are predominantly found in Morocco and Algeria, and more marginally in Tunisia and Libya.

Concerning *Egypt,* the overwhelming majority of Egyptians speak Arabic and share a very homogeneous culture. The country presents strikingly uniform patterns and lifestyles, characterized by an exceptionally dense juxtaposition of rural and urban life, unseen in any other Arab or North African country. Only Nubia, a region of southern Egypt lying at the Sudanese border, confers on the country an African feature, since its exclusively black population never mixed with the predominant white population. The Sinai and the Red Sea shores are inhabited only by a small population of nomads. Despite its population being predominantly Sunni Moslem, Egypt embraces the most important concentration of Christians in the Middle East, i.e. the Copts (approximately six million) who are the direct descendants of the Egyptians of the

Pharaonic era. In the Sudan, the only populations that came to be completely Islamicized and Arabized are the ones inhabiting the northern part of the country; those living south either remained Animist or became Christian. In the second half of the 20th century, a civil war raged for a long time between those two parts of the country.

In contrast, the countries of the *Fertile Crescent*, like the rest of the Middle East, comprise an exceptionally wide spectrum of geographic and human environments ranging from sedentary or semi-sedentary nomads to peasants in lofty mountains, including farmers on fertile plains and millennial city-dwellers. Largely prevalent, the Arabic language and culture unite the region's different populations. Nevertheless, despite the overwhelming predominance of Sunni Muslims, the countries of the Fertile Crescent also encompass several Moslem religious communities including Shia Muslims, as well as various heterodox Muslim sects and Christian churches. Such diversity of environments is precisely what accounts for the uniqueness of this region. The Kurds living in Iraq and Syria have often played a prominent role in the political life of their respective countries, unlike their peers in Turkey and Iran. Similarly, the Armenians who survived the Anatolia massacres have significant economical and political weight in Iraq, Syria, and Lebanon (particularly in Lebanon).

The *Arabian peninsula* is the third constituent of the Arab sphere. Owing to its geography and to its historical migratory outflows, the region is largely open to the Mesopotamian Basin and the Fertile Crescent. Moreover, due to the multiplicity of its geographic structures, the Arabian peninsula also encompasses a variety of human environments including nomads in the central desert, traders, fishermen, but also city-dwellers on the coasts of the

Red Sea and the Persian Gulf, and farmers in the Yemeni and Omani mountains bordering the Indian Ocean. While there exists an outright linguistic uniformity, the region comprises various Muslim communities: the population living on the western Saudi coastline, in Bahrain, Kuwait, and Yemen, partly adheres to Shia Islam, whereas the followers of conservative Wahhabism and of Ibadism can be found respectively in Saudi Arabia and Oman. The discovery of the peninsula's abundant oil resources in the 20th century, as we shall see, spurred some sweeping political and socio-economic transformations which were to affect the entire Middle East, as Saudi Arabia exerted, thereafter, a great influence on the Arab world and Muslim countries. This influence was disproportionate to the weight of the Saudi population and culture, and was wielded to the detriment of the other Arab countries, mainly Egypt, which had been playing a prominent role in the renaissance of the Arab world since the 19th century.

Owing to its physical, human, and cultural geography, the Middle East was the historic centre of the world's earliest human civilizations. Those mainly developed in Egypt, in the Syro-Lebanese coastal cities as well as in the Mesopotamian Basin region. The Middle East's geographic setting has turned it, over the millennia, into a focal intersection of civilizations. Such cultural, linguistic, and cultural interactions, which have long epitomized the Arab, Iranian, and Turkish worlds, still find expression today in the close linguistic and cultural connections between the Arab peoples and North Africa on the one hand, and between the Persian and Turkish peoples and the Indian continent and central Asia on the other. The age-old significance of the Middle East as a crossroads of civilizations is further evidenced by the major stages of its history – discussed in further detail below.

3

The Major Strata of Middle Eastern History

Our journey into the physical and human geography of the Middle East allowed us to measure the depth of its history and the richness of its cultural geology. Thus, it is now possible to examine the history of the Middle East, using the same methodology, by studying the historical evolution of the entities that dominated the region either simultaneously or successively. In order to reconstitute the history of the Middle East in all its splendour, it seemed more constructive to veer off from the standard periodization systems (Classical Antiquity, Middle Ages, Renaissance, etc.) which apply to European history, as well as from the political prism of historical analysis, which reflects Europe's own 'national' partitions. Continuing on with our analysis of the geology of cultures, we will approach the history of the Middle East by looking into the permanence of its major centres of civilization: Mesopotamia and the Fertile Crescent, Helleno-Turkish Anatolia, the Iranian plateaus, and Egypt.

This historical exploration shall bring us to the modern era to witness the transformation of the Middle East's four chief centres of culture and civilization, the former seats of prestigious empires, into sluggish stretches of land in sharp demographic, economic, military, and cultural decline. We shall also witness the rapid and implacable rise of Europe's cultural, political, and military ascendancy. In earlier times, the European continent had suffered its share of Eastern invasions, but thereafter, all through the 19th and 20th centuries, it was the East's turn to endure the colonial or neo-colonial weight of the European powers, in total helplessness given the permanence of its dynamics (to which we shall return).

It is indeed one of history's cruel ironies that the withdrawal of the European powers from the Middle East was immediately followed by the irruption of the American 'giant', a close ally of the newly founded state of Israel, engendered by the convulsions of European history. In 2003, Mesopotamia was invaded by U.S. armed forces, the presence of which was already extensive in light of the end of the Cold War and the liberation of Kuwait, which had been briefly occupied by Iraq in 1990. This highly consequential event brought profound repercussions which reverberated throughout the whole region. In any case, it plunged this cradle of ancient civilizations into a spiral of violence and chaos; indeed, far from putting an end to the ordeals of the region, this new incursion only aggravated them further.

Mesopotamian history (also called Babylonian, Chaldean, and Assyrian)

The Mesopotamian Basin, which extends to the Iranian plateau to the east, the Anatolian plateau to the north, and the Mediterranean shoreline to the west, is considered to be the cradle of sedentarization and urbanization. Together with the Nile Valley, the Mesopotamian Basin is the world's oldest producer of history and an archetype of the imperial structures which governed the Middle East and its different extensions in Europe, Asia, and Africa, from the 7th millennium BC until the collapse of the Ottoman Empire in 1919. Over the millennia, the Middle East's imperial structures have been incessantly broken down into small kingdoms and reassembled again into larger units. Imperial structures were short-lived, yet royal city-states did not prove more sustainable. The shock of migratory waves and the degradation of agricultural environments dictated the structuring and de-structuring of those political entities, whose centres of power tended to shift from the 'Semitic' South to the 'Aryan' North.

Ancient Mesopotamia and Chaldea (2370 BC–640 CE)

The Akkad (2370–2230 BC) and Ur (2111–2003 BC) empires

The Akkad Empire was founded after a Semitic invasion from the Arabian peninsula. It was built over the first Sumerian urban agglomerations (5th millennium BC) which developed at sites like Eridu, Uruk, Lagash, and Ur. Those first cities were destroyed between 3500 and 3000 BC. King Sargon was the foremost figure of this empire. His rule extended to the Mediterranean coastline, the Anatolian plateau, perhaps even reaching the borders of the Indian continent. The Akkad Empire collapsed after the invasion of a nomadic people known as the 'Gutians'. But this first empire was able to rise again at the close of the 3rd millennium BC, as the economy of Sumerian cities was largely left untouched. It even witnessed a remarkable flourishing of civil and commercial law, paving the way for the famous Hammurabi Code which appeared at the break of the 2nd millennium BC.

The Babylonian empires and kingdoms (1984–1694 BC and 1206–539 BC)

The gradual silting of the Mesopotamian Delta, the increase in its water salinity, and its infiltration by nomads, led the Akkado-Sumerian centres of power of the low basin to erode; central power re-emerged, consequently, further to the north, at Babylon, lying at the heart of the Mesopotamian Basin. As mentioned previously, King Hammurabi (c.1792–1750 BC) was the leading figure of the Babylonian Empire. He reunited Mesopotamia and devised an eponymous 'code' described as the 'foremost Babylonian legacy transmitted to civilization'.[4] Inscribed upon a high basalt stele currently exhibited at the Louvre Museum, this code provided a comprehensive set of laws regarding relations between the different social classes, commercial, financial, and land-property transactions, the organization of justice by the state, etc.

The Babylonian Empire began to decay with the arrival of new nomadic peoples into the region: the Kassites from the Iranian plateaus, the Elamites, whose origins are unknown and who settled in Chaldea (east of the Mesopotamian Basin), the Hittites and the Mitannians from Central Asia, the Aramaeans from the Syrian Desert, and the Assyrians from northern Mesopotamia. Nevertheless, Babylon continued to be a paramount imperial centre for the Kassites from 1571 to 1153 BC. Several Neo-Babylonian empires and kingdoms rose between 1206 and 538 BC. This was followed by a long period of decline due to raids by Aramaean tribes and to Assyrian domination right until the Chaldean dynasty seized the throne of Babylon. The Chaldeans ruled from 627 to 539 BC, during which they conquered Assyria to the north and the Syrian corridor all the way to Tyre. The foremost figure of this period is King Nebuchadnezzar II (605–562 BC).

---

[4] See Jacques Pirenne, *Les Grands Courants de l'histoire universelle*, vol. I (Paris: Editions de la Baconnière/Albin Michel, 1959), p. 31.

The Achaemenid, Parthian, and Sasanid empires and kingdoms (539 BC–640 CE)

From the 4th century BC until the 7th century CE, after the fall of the Babylonian and Assyrian empires, Mesopotamia and the countries of the Fertile Crescent were to be dominated, successively or simultaneously, by the Persians, Greeks, Romans, and Byzantines. In 539, Achaemenid king Cyrus entered Babylon and established Persian domination over the Mesopotamian Basin. The Achaemenid Empire however adopted Aramaic as its official language, providing further evidence of the constant cultural interplay in the Middle East. The Seleucid Greeks succeeded the Achaemenids but neglected the Babylonian capital. Following the Seleucid interlude, the Mesopotamian Basin remained under Persian rule, as the Parthians, followed by the Sasanids – who established their capital at Ctesiphon, near modern Baghdad – reigned supreme until the arrival of the Arabs in 640. But it was not until the advent of the Baghdad caliphate that Mesopotamia recovered its status as a political centre of power of 'Semitic' influence.

Assyrian northern Mesopotamia (2000–500 BC)

Assyria refers to the middle and northern parts of the Mesopotamian Valley, which was populated originally by the Sumerians. Assyria's political history, just like its cosmogony and deities, is closely linked to that of the Sumerian empires and dynasties. The first great city in history bears the name of its king-god, Ashur (around 2500 BC). Between the 20th and the 18th centuries BC, Assyria became a vital trade centre for the entire Mesopotamian area, but was later torn asunder by the dynastic quarrels between the Sumerian kings and the Amorite tribal chiefs who campaigned from Ashur and reached Cappadocia, Anatolia, and Lebanon. However, the unstable life of the first empire (14th–12th centuries BC) made it an easy target for invasions by the Aramaean tribes of the Syrian Desert and the Elamite tribes of the Iranian plateaus. The second empire (9th–7th centuries BC) readopted an expansionist policy and conquered the Fertile Crescent, the island of Cyprus, and Egypt in 671 BC. The two major figures of this empire were King Sargon II (722–705 BC), Sharru-kin in Assyrian, and Ashurbanipal (669–626 BC) who settled in Nineveh.

But it was the Medes, a nomadic people of Indo-Iranian descent, who ultimately overthrew Assyrian power in the Middle East. The Assyrians were famous for the violence of their conquests, their dynastic disputes, and their extremely strict penal code (which included mutilations and whippings), particularly towards women. Assyrian civilization was more brutal than the Sumero-Babylonian of the lower Mesopotamian Valley, but both civilizations were closely linked to each other by human origins, language, and social structures.

With the downfall of the Assyrian entity, northern Mesopotamia ceased to host any autonomous political structures. The Greeks, Turks, Iranians, not counting the Armenians – who were once significant in number but are now extinct (see below) – struggled for many centuries for mastery of Assyrian lands and their geographic extensions, at the confluence of the Anatolian mountains and Azerbaijan. Adjoined to Iraq in 1924, this region is presently largely populated by the Kurds, a people of Indo-European lineage, who were left without a country after the colonial partitions of the Middle East, although the Treaty of Sèvres signed in 1921 provided for the constitution of a Kurdish political entity.

The Fertile Crescent and the Syro-Mesopotamian entity

Phoenician cities and small 'Semitic' kingdoms (2nd–1st millennia BC)

Phoenician cities reached their zenith in the 2nd millennium BC. Ras Shamra (near Latakia in Syria), Byblos (Jbeil), located in the heart of the Lebanese littoral, and Tyre (Sour), lying at its southern edge, were important ports that played a fundamental role in the Middle Eastern economy. The Phoenicians founded many trading posts across the Mediterranean coastline, the most famous of which was Carthage around 814 BC. As put by geographer Élisée Reclus, 'Thanks to their geographic explorations, their sailing to distant lands around Europe and Africa, their journeys inland and through rivers, as well as their supplying and introduction of metal, wood, gum, cloth, clay, and many other manufactured artefacts later discovered by archaeologists at numerous sites, the Phoenicians prepared the western forest tribes for forthcoming civilization by establishing trade-links between them. Indeed, the world owes much to the Phoenicians for the ushering in of a prehistoric transition without which history, strictly speaking, would never have begun in the European world.'[5]

An exhaustive historical description of the tribes of Israel can be found in the Bible; it is therefore unnecessary to review it here in full detail. The Philistines came with the Sea Peoples and struggled against the Israelites for many years (12th–11th centuries BC). Towards 1000 BC, David established the Kingdom of Israel. However, the Israelite power began to wane no later than the 9th century BC due

[5] See Élisée Reclus, *Nouvelle Géographie Universelle*, vol. IX (Paris, 1884).

to the eruption of internal quarrels and the increasing influence of the Assyrians who conquered the entire Fertile Crescent region in the 8th century BC.

The Kingdom of Palmyra (1st–3rd century CE) was also one of the small 'Semitic' kingdoms of the Middle East. Made famous by Queen Zenobia's strong personality and beauty, this kingdom was a remarkable synthesis of Greek and Aramaean cultures. Another significant entity was the Nabataean Kingdom of Petra (between Amman and the Aqaba Gulf), which was also a synthesis of Greek and Arab cultures which spanned from the 3rd century BC to the beginning of the 1st century CE. The extent to which these kingdoms were able to develop in utterly desert parts of the Fertile Crescent is simply remarkable. Last but not least, an important rural settlement arose in the limestone massif of northern Syria between the 2nd and 7th centuries CE, as evidenced by the remainders of around seven hundred villages.[6]

Roman and Greek conquests

Following the definitive decline of Phoenician civilization marked by the fall of Carthage, the major centre of Phoenician military power, to the Roman army in 146 BC, the Syro-Palestinian ensemble came intermittently under Egyptian and Persian rule. It came under the control of Alexander the Great in 333 BC, before yielding to the Roman Empire. The Romans defeated the Carthaginians in North Africa (148–146 BC) and conquered Egypt (47 BC) and later the Syro-Mesopotamian ensemble.

---

[6] See Georges Tate, *Les Campagnes de la Syrie du Nord du IIe au VIIe siècle* (Paris: Librairie orientaliste Paul Geuthner, 1992).

The Middle East thus fell into the hands of the Eastern Roman Empire, which became progressively, as of the 5th century CE, the Byzantine Empire, a cultural and political synthesis of Greek and Roman cultures. Roman rule endured until the Arab invasions in 634, which compelled Byzantine power to retreat to the Anatolian Plateau and effectively erased it from North Africa as of 659 CE. The eastern part of the Mediterranean thereafter remained under direct Greco-Roman domination for approximately 900 years. As previously mentioned, this period of Greco-Roman rule, which has become lost in the mists of time, has had a profound impact on the societies and cultures of the region. The prestigious architectural vestiges found in all the Mediterranean Arab countries and in Turkey bear witness to this seminal presence.

The Arab conquest and the Umayyad and Abbasid caliphates (659–945)

In the wake of the Islamic monotheistic prophecy, the Arab conquerors effectively annihilated Persian power and caused the Byzantine Empire, then ruling in Egypt, North Africa, and the Mediterranean façade of the Fertile Crescent, to recede gradually. At the outset, four caliphs called the 'rightly guided caliphs' succeeded the Prophet Muhammad who had settled in Medina (632–650). The caliphate was then transferred to Damascus for about a century (see below), before being transferred to Baghdad under the Abbasid Dynasty.

The Muslim caliphs, readapting an Assyro-Babylonian terminology, aspired to be the 'vicars of God on earth' (on the spiritual level), but also to ensure the temporal succession of the Prophet. However, the reign of Arab caliphs was comparatively short-lived with respect to the history of the Middle East, as it lasted merely three and a half centuries. Abbasid rule was prolonged nominally in Cairo under the protection of the Mamluk State until the Ottoman conquest in the 16th century, although the Abbasid caliphs had already been ousted from Baghdad, which was destroyed by the Mongols in 1258 (see below).

The political power gained by the Arabs though their remarkable military campaigns extending as far as the Iberian Peninsula westwards and much of central Asia eastwards, was exhausted very rapidly with the eruption of violent dynastic clashes over the succession of the Prophet. Such conflicts brought about the schism between Sunni and Shia Muslims, which persists to this day. While the Sunnites acknowledged the order and legitimacy of caliphal successions from outside the Prophet's family, the Shiites, the partisans of Ali (the fourth caliph: 656–661), cousin and son-in-law of the Prophet, believed that caliphal succession belonged strictly to the Prophet and his direct descendants.

It was under the Umayyad Caliphate of Damascus (659–750) that the Muslim conquerors subjugated North Africa and the Iberian Peninsula, the Fertile Crescent and its Mediterranean coastline, and Iran. The Abbasid Caliphate reinstated Mesopotamia to its earlier grandeur and made a capital of Baghdad, a new city founded in 762, thirty kilometres away from Babylon. The Abbasids, who were the direct descendants of the Prophet, were propelled to power by a coalition of Arabs hostile to the Umayyad Dynasty (a dynasty not related to the Prophet's direct lineage nor that of his close companions), and Iranians from the province of Khorasan. This coalition presented itself as a rigorist reinstatement of Islam. Yet, it was under the Abbasids, in particular under the caliphates of Harun al-Rashid (786–

809) and al-Ma'mun (814–833), that this Arab Empire reached its zenith, bringing arts, literature, philosophy, and science to uncharted heights. Arab culture indeed embraced the legacy of the Greek philosophers, which was later passed onto Europe via Arab Spain: religious freedom and philosophy flourished, as was the case with poetry, music, medicine, and astronomy.

Nevertheless, this brilliant empire started to show signs of weakness from the very beginning of its existence, due to the eruption of persistent quarrels between Shiites and Sunnites, to the birth of numerous religious sects veering off the official Sunni and Shia dogmas, and to the increasing prominence of the Turkish and Iranian praetorian guards. From the end of the 9th century until the consolidation of Ottoman dominion, those guards acted as independent yet rival centres of power (kingdoms, principalities, sultanates), depriving the caliphs of any effective authority. Such dynasties included the Buyids, Shia Iranians from the Dayalman Mountains in Iran (932–1055) who conquered Baghdad in 945; the Samanids, another Iranian dynasty (874–999); the Tulunids in Egypt and Syria (868–905); and the Hamdanids, an Arab dynasty that governed northern Syria from Aleppo (929–1003). The end of the 9th century in Mesopotamia and the Arabian peninsula also witnessed the famous Zanj (black slaves) Rebellion (869–883), followed by the insurrection of the Ismaili Qarmatians (a doctrine derived from Shiism).

In 1055, the Seljuq Turks captured Baghdad and reinstated Sunnism as the official dogma, but their power also declined shortly afterwards. On February 10, 1258, Mongol leader Hulagu razed Baghdad to the ground and executed the last nominally ruling Abbasid caliph; a part of his family had already fled to Cairo and managed to survive. Consequently,

Mesopotamia re-entered a period of uninterrupted decline: long coveted by and contested between the Turkish Sunnite and Iranian Shiite dynasties, Baghdad's importance waned thereafter. A mere provincial city under the Ottoman Empire in the 18th century, Baghdad only regained prominence when it became capital of modern Iraq under British occupation. By then, however, the peoples of the Fertile Crescent and those of the Syrian, Lebanese, Palestinian, and Egyptian coastlines, had been completely culturally Arabized. The Aramaeans, Chaldeans, Syriacs, and Assyrians of the former Persian, Neo-Babylonian, and Assyrian empires, as well as Egypt, forged the Classical Arab culture still practised today. Although Arabic was the language of Koranic revelation, the different Christian Churches of the local populations that were converted to Christianity by the apostles massively embraced Arabic language and culture, at varying paces in the different regions. The variants of Aramaic (quite similar to Arabic) and Greek (prevalent since the conquest of Alexander the Great) were thus relegated to mere liturgical languages.

Under Arab domination, Andalusia suffered a similar fate to that of the Syro-Mesopotamian ensemble. In 699, North Africa was conquered in the name of the Umayyad Caliphate of Damascus, to the detriment of the Byzantine Empire. In 711, the Arabo-Berber armies crossed the Strait of Gibraltar – an Arabic short form of the word mountain (*jabal*) and the name of the military chief of the expedition (*Tarik*). Established in the Iberian Peninsula with Cordova as its capital, this emirate gained independence from Abbasid trusteeship, which had succeeded the Umayyad Caliphate in 773. Under this Andalusian caliphate of Umayyad origin, philosophy, religion, and science (astronomy and medicine in particular) flourished with prominent figures such as philosophers Ibn Rushd, also called Averroës (1126–1198);

Ibn Maymun, also called Maimonides (Jewish philosopher, 1135–1204); and the eminent mystic-philosopher, Ibn Arabi (1165–1240); as well as two renowned travellers, Ibn Jubayr (1145–1217) and Ibn Battutah (1304–1377), who both wrote celebrated accounts of their journeys; and not least, the world's very first sociologist, Ibn Khaldun (1332–1406).

Nevertheless, the Umayyad Caliphate of Cordova suffered the same decadence as the Abbasid Caliphate. The violent internal quarrels that beset the Umayyad Caliphate led it to collapse, at the close of the 11th century, into small principalities that fell into the hands of several contending warlords. This decadence favoured the rise of the Spanish Reconquista, which gained momentum thereafter: Toledo was lost in 1085, Cordoba in 1236, and Seville in 1248. In 1492, both Arabs and Jews were cast out of the Iberian peninsula for good.

The history of Anatolia

The Hittites (165–1200 BC)

The first traces of the Hittites in the Anatolian Plateau are extremely old and date back to the years 2300–2200 BC, but they succumbed to an invasion by an Indo-European people that kept the name 'Hittite'. Hittite dominion was made famous by the conquest of Pharaonic Egypt and Assyria (13th century BC). In the 12th century BC, their power was shattered by the Dorians, who settled shortly afterwards in Anatolia. The Dorians formed one of the human constituents of Greek civilization. Smaller royal entities were subsequently created in Syria, but they were abolished by the Assyrian kings in the 8th century BC.

The Greek Middle East (from the 2nd millennium BC to the 16th century CE)

The history of Mesopotamia and Assyria has introduced us to the peoples of the Anatolian high plateau: the Hittites and the Dorians, the ancestors of the Greeks. We also saw the influence of the Mesopotamian and Egyptian civilizations on the development of Greek culture. From the beginning of the 2nd millennium BC until the fall of the Byzantine Empire in 1453, the Greek presence in the Middle East constitutes a fundamental historical fact that official histories do not emphasize enough. When Europe annexed the Greek heritage to its own cultural patrimony, contemporary Iranian, Arab, and Turkish cultures simply erased all memory relating to that heritage. In reality, however, Asia Minor and the Mediterranean coastline had provided Greek history and culture with a solid foothold since the founding of Troy. The Middle East's Greek heritage, with the exception of the incessant wars with the Persians and Alexander's fulgurant conquests, was mainly incarnated by the lengthy period of Byzantine rule, which was immediately followed by the Ottoman Empire.

Aegean civilizations (20th–12th centuries BC)

The Aegean civilizations of the 20th to 12th centuries BC were eminent maritime and mercantile civilizations that fostered close relations with Egypt, Assyria, and Mesopotamia, as well as the Phoenician cities of the Syro-Lebanese littoral. The islands of the Aegean Sea were invaded by a number of different peoples today known by the civilizations they created. First there was the Cretan civilization (2000–1700 BC), followed by its Achaean peer (also known as the Mycenaean civilization) between the 17th and 13th centuries BC, named after an Indo-European people, the Achaeans. The Cretans and the Achaeans founded the first cities in Asia Minor and Cilicia (Troy, Colophon, Ephesus, Priene, Miletus, etc.).

The Dorian invasions and the rise of Greek power (12th–5th centuries BC)

In the 12th century BC, the Dorian invasions (of Indo-European origins) cast a shadow on Greek civilization, but increased the number of settlers in Thrace and Asia Minor as far as the Black Sea, paving the way for the colonization of Italy as of the 8th century BC, and of the Libyan coasts. Greek expansion was put to a halt by the rise of Persian power, which resulted in the long sequence of Greco–Persian wars over control of the Middle East. It is during those years that the famous Battle of Marathon (490) was fought.

The Empire of Alexander (336–275) and the eastern Hellenistic monarchies

In the 5th and 4th centuries BC, the Greek world was torn apart by violent hegemonic struggles between its different cities. The epic journey of Alexander the Great against the Persians started in Macedonia at the end of the 4th century BC. In 334 BC, Alexander undertook an expedition to reconquer Asia Minor and Egypt. The Greek army first recovered all of Asia Minor's coastal cities and then traversed the littoral all the way to Egypt, putting an end to Persian hegemony and founding Alexandria. From Egypt, Alexander marched on to conquer Persia. The Achaemenid Empire was effectively overthrown at the Battle of Arbela in 331 BC.

Persepolis was shattered and the armies of Alexander acclaimed as liberators in Babylonia, where the conqueror established his capital, Susa. After five years of military campaigning, Alexander reached the edge of the Ganges River, in the heart of the Indian continent. Exhausted, his troops refused to advance further. He reached central Asia, as far as modern Samarqand, and then travelled back to the south of the Indian peninsula. Alexander succumbed to fatigue in Susa, in 323 BC, at the age of thirty-three.

Only the Arab conquest in much later years was to match the military prowess of Alexander's epic journey, with similar fast and ephemeral conquests leaving an enduring cultural impact on each subjugated land. The Middle East was to remain under Greek dominion until the arrival of the Romans in the 1st century BC. Upon Alexander's death, his lieutenants gradually split his empire. In the Middle East, Ptolemy won Egypt and founded his own dynasty; Antigonus got Asia Minor (which later became the Kingdom of Pergamum which fell into the hands of the Romans in 126 BC); and Seleucus obtained Mesopotamia and the Fertile Crescent, where he founded the Seleucid Dynasty whose rule extended to Asia Minor. The Roman armies of Pompey ultimately overthrew the Seleucid Dynasty in 64 BC while the troops of Octavian defeated the Ptolemaic Dynasty of Egypt in 30 BC.

The Byzantine Empire (395–1453)

The lengthy rule of the Byzantine Empire was preceded by Roman rule in Greece which gradually extended to Asia Minor and the Fertile Crescent (as shown earlier). At the advent of Christianity, this vast area of the Middle East consisted of provinces under Roman administration. The

Roman Empire was at its pinnacle at that time, but the eastern provinces were growing increasingly influential; Emperor Septimius Severus (193–211 CE) originally came from the Libyan coast, while Emperor Philip known as the Arabian (244–249) came from Syria. Under Emperor Constantine (306–337), who acknowledged the Christian religion, the Roman Empire in fact yielded to the Orient – Christianity's native land – thereby laying the foundations of the Byzantine Empire with the founding of Constantinople (330), where his son, Constans, established the capital of the empire.

Just like Islam to caliphates, Christianity was often the cause of much of the weakness and the unrest that beset the Byzantine Empire. While adopting Greek culture, then prominent in Asia Minor, the Byzantines perpetuated the Roman Empire which was seriously undermined by the Barbarian invasions in its western part. The disputes regarding the divine or human nature of Christ, the Trinity and the role of the Holy Spirit, as well as the autonomy of the patriarchal Church Sees, divided the Byzantine provinces and eventually totally separated the Byzantine Church (also called Orthodox) from the Roman Catholic Church. But the latter persisted in its will to prove the ascendancy of the Roman Papal See with respect to other chief Patriarchates, mainly the See of the Byzantine Empire, Constantinople. The schism between the two chief Churches was consummated in 1054. Over the centuries, this East–West rivalry reached such heights that the Fourth Crusade, initially designed to conquer the Holy Land, was deviated from its original purpose and directed against the Byzantine Empire. In 1204, Constantinople was invaded and pillaged by the Crusaders, and the Empire shared between the Venetians and the Franks. Despite being considerably weakened, the Empire managed to rise again in Asia Minor, south of the Black Sea, at Trebizond and Nicaea, where the Byzantines concocted their re-conquest of Constantinople, which took place in 1261. But the exhausted Empire eventually expired in 1453 when the capital was definitively subjugated by the Ottoman Turks.

The prevalent social and cultural fabric under the Byzantine Empire renders it typically Middle Eastern. Indeed, the Byzantine Empire shares numerous common features found in all typical Middle Eastern entities (Persian, Mesopotamian, and Egyptian): the indefectible loyalty to the past incarnated by the Classical Greek legacy; the adoption of Caesaropapism (a political system in which the Emperor is also the supreme head of the Church, and devises doctrines that become state laws); the perpetuation of the legal traditions that made Byzantine Law, and particularly the Theodosian (*Codex Theodosianus*) and Justinian (*Corpus Juris Civilis*) codes, a synthesis of Roman, Mesopotamian, and Assyrian Law; and lastly, the predominance of agnatic kinship (which favoured patrilineality, i.e. the father's lineage).

However, the structure of the monotheistic and prophetic religions was less adequate than Classical Greek or Babylonian paganism, to the expression of sub-cultures, which are vital to any human society. That is why the Byzantine Empire was to struggle constantly against the 'heresies' developing in its provinces. But the Byzantine Church would never succeed at abolishing Monophysitism (belief in Christ having only one nature, this being purely divine) and Nestorianism (belief in Christ having two distinct natures). The first doctrine cemented the autonomy of the Egyptian Church against Byzantine dominion, and that of the Armenian Church as well; it would find many followers in Syria and in Ancient Assyria (the Jacobites).

Nestorianism, on the other hand, created the unique Mesopotamian and Chaldean Christian rites, which prospered and extended as far as India and China.

Yet these Christological quarrels grew increasingly brutal and violent, thereby paving the way for the Arab invasion of Syria, Mesopotamia, Armenia, Palestine, and Egypt. The Arab conquerors, who shared close cultural features with the peoples of the Byzantine provinces (with the exception of Egypt) and were the harbingers of a new form of monotheism, were welcomed with a sense of relief almost everywhere. The extreme tolerance to Christians that characterized the Arab conquest at its outset alleviated the acute religious tensions that had defined those regions up till then. In Damascus and Jerusalem, Christians and Muslims shared churches and prayed together; in 638, Caliph Omar entered Jerusalem and displayed a great deal of modesty and respect towards the religious authorities.

Islam thereby began its religious conquest of that part of the Middle East. Nonetheless, it rapidly grew stricter when internal conflicts arose between the followers of the Prophet's son-in-law, Ali (the fourth caliph), and his assassinated or abducted successors, bringing about an escalation of religious rigorism. Ultimately, Christianity began to shrink with the implementation of jurisprudence provisions hindering the practice of Christian cults (often inspired by the Byzantine or Persian edicts against unofficial cults), and the increase of non-Muslim taxes. However, Christianity was permitted to retain the diversity of its churches, which have all maintained their autonomy and specificities (despite the Byzantine Empire's failed attempts) until the present day.

The Byzantine Empire successfully halted Arab expansion in northern Syria, sometimes even recovering certain lands.

It was much later that the Empire finally collapsed due to the blows of the Crusades and to the implacable advance of the Ottoman Turks.

The Armenians in the Middle East

The Armenians came to the Middle East in the 12th century BC, during the Indo-European invasions that put an end to Hittite domination. Their features began to take shape around the 7th century BC after they gained their independence from the Greeks and the Persians in 190 BC. Under Tigranes the Great, the Armenians extended their rule to the mountains of the Caucasus and eastern Anatolia as far as the Syrian coast. The first Armenian kingdom was short-lived as it faded with the Roman conquest at the beginning of the Christian era. A second empire (reigning 9th–11th centuries CE) was established, under the Bagrationi Dynasty.

However, combined attacks by the Seljuq Turks and the Byzantines, in addition to interior dissensions among the feudal Armenians led this empire to disintegrate. Until the start of the 20th century, the Armenians remained a vibrant constituent of the Middle East, their geographic implantation stretching from the southern Caucasian region to northern Syria and the Mediterranean shoreline. But during World War I, the Armenian people fell victim to the miscalculations of the Allies and to the jolts of the disarrayed Ottoman army. They were massacred and massively deported to the Soviet Union and the Arab countries in a series of events that deeply marked the Middle East.

The slow conquest of the Middle East by the Seljuq Turks

After having played a paramount role in Chinese history, the Turks, who came originally from Siberia and the plains of central Asia, turned to the Middle East, where they established their first state in the 10th century CE, in the Iranian Caucasus region. Despite this being a Muslim state, the Turks long practised Manichaeism and Nestorianism. Their first significant empire was that of the Ghaznavids (962–1040), whose rule stretched to the Iranian borders, as far as Afghanistan and India. Their settlement in Asia Minor took place under the Seljuqs, the descendants of the Oghuz tribes settled near the Aral Sea. After overthrowing the Ghaznavids in 1038–1040, Toghril Beg, the founder of the Seljuq Dynasty, set sights on the possessions of the Abbasid caliphate. The Seljuqs conquered Baghdad in 1055, thus putting an end to the Iranian Buyids, and then invaded Syria and the bulk of Armenia in 1054–1055.

Alp-Arslan (1063–1072) was one of the foremost Seljuq sultans. He invaded Georgia and completed the conquest of Armenia and Syria. His troops defeated the Byzantine Empire in 1071 at the battle of Manzikert, which represented the most crushing and disastrous military defeat ever suffered by the Byzantines. Not only did this battle break Byzantine resistance, but it also tightened the Seljuq grip on the Middle East. Another famous Seljuq figure was Sultan Malik-Shah (1073–1092), who extended Seljuq rule to central Asia. His reign also witnessed the emergence of the 'Assassin' sect, an offshoot of Shiite Ismailism. The Assassins were made famous by their struggle against Sunni Seljuq authority through the practice of large-scale political assassinations. The fortress of Alamut, lying on the high Iranian plateaus, constituted the stronghold of this sect. The

Seljuqs – just like the Mamluks and later the Ottomans – entrenched Sunni Islam everywhere and warded off Shiism that had hitherto flourished greatly under the Buyids and the Fatimids of Egypt. And just like the Ottomans later on, the Seljuqs maintained the autonomy and the privileges granted to the Christian and Jewish communities of the Middle East.

By the 12th century, the Seljuq Sultanate had spread its dominion over all of Anatolia and the Mediterranean coast. Byzantium had virtually nothing left in Asia, save the coasts of the Black Sea. Several Turkish leaders, called the Mamluks, governed Egypt and numerous Syrian regions. They strived to eradicate the Shia movement, which was still quite active in that part of the Middle East. The 13th century witnessed the rise to power of the descendants of a Turkmen tribe, the Ottomans, who gradually succeeded the Seljuqs. Osman, the son of a tribe leader and Seljuq vassal named Ertugrul, is regarded as the founder of the Ottoman Dynasty around 1280. He extended his rule at the expense of the Byzantines through the conquest of the coasts of the Black Sea.

The advance of the large Turkmen tribes that had been halted by a succession of Crusades (see below), the expansion of Egypt, and the Mongol invasions, resumed under this new dynasty. Under Murad I (1360–1389), the Ottomans extended their conquests in Anatolia and advanced on Europe, where they raided the Balkans from Thrace. The battle of Kosovo (1389) against the Serbs was decisive: Murad I was killed in combat, but his son Bayezid took command of the Ottoman troops and led them to victory. He succeeded his father as Sultan and provided the Empire with the necessary institutions to consolidate its rule – he reigned until 1402. Insurgence was the order of the day under Bayezid. He was confronted with many rebellious

Turkish tribes, but also with the emergence of Timur (Timurlenk/Tamerlane), who re-conquered Mesopotamia in 1394 and diminished the might of the Mamluks of Syria.

Bayezid also faced another Crusade, called for by Pope Boniface IX. Made up of contingents from different European countries (the English, Scottish, Bohemians, Austrians, and Italians), this Crusade was successfully repelled and defeated by Bayezid at Nicopolis in 1396. In 1402, however, the Mongol army of Timur overcame the Ottoman troops at Ankara, in the heart of the Anatolian plateaus, and Bayezid was held prisoner. He died in captivity in 1403; two years later, the Mongol conqueror also passed away.

Following an interlude of about a decade, the dismembered Ottoman Empire was reunified and expanded under Mehmed I (1413–1421). The Byzantine capital, Constantinople, was conquered in 1453 by Sultan Mehmed II (1451–1481) after a 54-day siege. Instead of pillaging the city, he reasserted the patriarch's authority over the Christian population, which allowed the Christians to keep their possessions. Renamed Istanbul, this city became the capital of the Empire in 1457. The Ottomans then turned to Moldavia, Walachia, and the Crimea, thus making their domination over the Black Sea complete.

It was not until the 16th century that Ottoman sultans undertook the conquest of the Iranian and Arab parts of the Middle East. Between 1512 and 1517, Azerbaijan, western Anatolia, Kurdistan, and Armenia, followed by Syria, Egypt (where they put an end to Mamluk power), and North Africa fell into their hands. The Ottoman Empire reached its zenith under Sultan Süleyman called 'the Lawgiver' (1521–1586), also known as 'the Magnificent'. He set afoot a remarkable administrative

apparatus that aroused the admiration and envy of the
European sovereigns.[7] It was also in 1529, during the
European expansion, that the Ottoman armed forces
besieged Vienna for the first time – albeit unsuccessfully.
Their second attempt in 1683 also failed, as the Empire
had been falling into military decline since the great naval
battle of Lepanto (1571). Fought on the coasts of the
Adriatic, this crucial battle allowed the European fleets to
definitively assert their superiority over their Turkish peers.
In 1699, the peace treaty of Karlowitz permanently shifted
Hungary from Ottoman to Austrian control. It also
ushered the beginning of the end of the Ottoman Empire,
now reeling under the weight of the double Russian and
Austrian pressures that were to be wielded uninterruptedly
over this last large political and imperial entity – the
inheritor of all the cultural strata which formed throughout
the long history of the Middle East.

The Ottoman Empire thus became the 'sick man' of
Europe. At the peak of their colonial expansion, the
European powers became embroiled between themselves in
fierce struggles over mastery of the Middle East. Such
European dissensions postponed the demise of the Ottoman
Empire until the end of World War I, when the Allies entered
victorious into Istanbul, Jerusalem, Damascus, and Baghdad.

---

[7] See Lucette Valensi, *Venise et la Sublime Porte* (Paris: Hachette Litteratures, 2005).

The Crusades in the Middle East (1096–1291) and the Mongol Conquests (1227–1260)

The nine Crusades and their aftermath

The Crusades are a poignant episode that has marked the consciousness of Europeans and Middle Easterners alike. Unlike the Byzantines, Turks, and Iranians, who were all natives to the region, the Crusaders came from distant lands to found new kingdoms and to abolish the newly born monotheistic religion, Islam, portrayed as a figure of the Antichrist. This stage of Middle Eastern history spanned for a considerable two centuries. Historian Georges Tate, a Byzantium expert, describes this period as being a 'two-hundred-year epic that pitted powerful and audacious figures against each other and resulted, unquestionably, in a climate of mutual hostility, distrust, and a lack of understanding that spanned for many centuries'.[8]

Crusading emerged as Christian Europe's tardy response to the Arabo-Berber invasion of the Iberian Peninsula. Indeed, the Crusades were only launched after the decline of Arab Muslim dominion and the start of the *Reconquista* in the Iberian peninsula. The Muslim hold on the island of Sicily was also brought to an end by the Norman invasions. But crusading also resulted from Europe's domestic evolutions, mainly to polish the Papacy's tarnished image and weakened authority, after its quarrels with the ruling political elites. The Papacy used the Holy War outside the

---

[8] See Georges Tate, *L'Orient des croisades* (Paris: Gallimard, 1991). As we shall see in the second section, the climate of distrust that prevailed then was later exacerbated by several historical events. Those included the expansion of European colonialism, the creation of the state of Israel in 1948, the invasion of Afghanistan in 2001, and the occupation of Iraq in 2003 by the United States and their European allies.

continent to halt the rise of temporal power in Europe.[9] The Byzantine Empire – severely defeated at the battle of Manzikert in 1071 by the troops of Seljuq sultan Alp-Arslan – also appealed to the Pope and the Christian sovereigns of Europe for aid in order to resist the Turkish threat. During the Crusades, Latin Kingdoms were established in the East, mainly at Edessa, Antioch, Tripoli, Jerusalem, and Cyprus. However, these kingdoms were short-lived, surviving only through Western reinforcements and fragile alliances with the local Muslim sultans and princes.

There were seven main expeditions. Pope Urban II called for the first one on November 27, 1095, at the Council of Clermont. The First Crusade was launched in 1096. In 1099, the Crusaders conquered Jerusalem where they established a kingdom, after having conquered Edessa and Antioch, and established them as earldoms. After the Turks recovered the earldom of Edessa in 1144, a second Crusade was launched under the commands of Louis VII and Conrad III. But the tenuous relations with the Byzantine Empire complicated the advance of new European armies. As a result, this Crusade suffered several consecutive losses until its final defeat in 1149. It was not until 1189 that the Third Crusade was launched in response to the capture of Jerusalem in 1187 by the Ayyubid Sultan of Egypt, Saladin, who was of Kurdish descent. This expedition was led by Europe's most prestigious sovereigns: Richard I (Richard the Lion-Heart), Philip II Augustus, and the Germanic Emperor Fredrick I (Frederick Barbarossa, whose drowning during this expedition resulted in the German retreat). The Crusaders subjugated Acre in

---

[9] See the benchmark work by Claude Cahen, *Orient et Occident au temps des croisades* (Paris: Aubier, 1983).

Palestine but failed to recover Jerusalem. This expedition is considered to have ended in 1191.

The Fourth Crusade, launched by the Venetians in 1202, left a dark stain in the memories of Eastern Christians, as it was diverted from its original goal to instead raid and sack Constantinople, the capital of the Byzantine Empire. This expedition ended in 1204. It led to the creation of an Eastern Latin Empire (1204–1261), while the siege of the Byzantine Empire was transferred to Nicaea. After this Crusade, the rupture between Western and Eastern Christianity was so irreversible that, in the 15th century, the Byzantines chose to open and yield their capital, Constantinople, to Turkish Sultan Mehmed II, rather than appeal again for the aid of the Roman Church.

The Fifth Crusade was rather longer than the previous ones (1217–1221). It was called for by Pope Innocent III in 1215, at the Fourth Council of Lateran. This Crusade was also somewhat sidetracked from its initial purpose – the conquest of Jerusalem – and instead tried conquering Egypt, albeit unsuccessfully. The same sidetracking happened to Seventh Crusade (1248–1254) as it unsuccessfully attempted to conquer Egypt; Louis IX, King of France, was held captive during this Crusade in 1250, along with his two brothers, and a costly ransom was paid for their release. In fact, the Sixth Crusade (1228–1229) had already succeeded in the peaceful recovery of Jerusalem, but it was led by Germanic Emperor Fredrick II and had been launched without the consent or the military support of the Pope, who had excommunicated Fredrick II. The peace treaty of Jaffa (1229) signed between Sultan Al-Kamil and Fredrick II granted Muslims the right to administer their own Holy Places. However, in 1244, Jerusalem was re-conquered by the forces of the Turkish army.

In 1270, Louis IX (the future Saint Louis) waged the Eighth Crusade, a military fiasco that cost him his life. In 1271, King Edward I of England led the Ninth and last Crusade, which was equally unsuccessful. As of 1268, the Principality of Antioch was taken over by the Turks; the latter recaptured the earldoms of Tripoli in 1289, and Acre in 1291, thereby effectively eliminating Christian Europe's political presence from the East, save for Cyprus where it lingered on for another three centuries until the island was conquered by the Ottomans. From a human standpoint, however, this presence survived in the numerous European families that settled in the Levant. Some converted to Islam and became linguistically Arabized; others remained Christian and turned to one of the local Eastern Churches, while embracing the local language and traditions.

This was a stormy period. It was marked by a series of hostilities followed by truces and friendly alliances between contending European kings, princes, and earls, and rival Turkish or Arab princes, kings, and sultans. The local Christian communities suffered most, torn between their affinities with the Muslims and the call of the Crusaders to repel Islam and to restore the political sovereignty of Christianity in the East.

In fact, from the beginning of the 13th century, both the Europeans and the Turks were confronted with the growing Mongol menace. Under such conditions, the Latin states of the East created during the Crusades had little chance of surviving. Shortly afterwards – as we shall see – in order to halt the advance of Ottoman power in Europe, other Crusades – albeit much shorter – were to be waged in an attempt to expel this ominous presence from Thrace and the Balkans.

The Mongol invasions

The Middle East had not yet recovered from the disruption of the Crusades when it found itself confronted with the Mongol invasions coming from central Asia and the Iranian corridors. Two historic figures are synonymous with these invasions and the sweeping changes they brought to the East. The first was Temuchin (1167–1227): after uniting the Mongol tribes in 1197 and being proclaimed their ruler, he undertook an expedition at the age of fifty-four to conquer the world. In 1206, he conquered the Asiatic steppes and was acknowledged as emperor under the name Genghis Khan. He then advanced on China – Beijing was conquered and sacked in 1215 – and central Asia, which was under the sovereignty of the Khwarezm Sultanate that had succeeded the Seljuq Empire. City after city was stormed: all of eastern Iran, then stretching from Afghanistan to the Indian borders, was conquered and the many Turkish and Iranian sultanates destroyed (1223–1224). In 1220 and 1221, Bukhara, Samarqand, and Nishapur were razed to the ground by the troops of Genghis Khan. In 1222, the Mongol armies reached the southern Russian steppes and the Caucasus.

Upon Genghis Khan's death in 1227, his son, Ogadai, assumed the command of the expeditions in 1235. In 1243, he sealed the disintegration of the Seljuq Empire, which was merely left with Anatolia, and then marched on Russia, Ukraine, Hungary, the Balkans, and the Caucasus. He crossed the Danube River in 1241, and conquered the city of Belgrade. The implacable Mongol conquests only came to an end with the death of Ogadai that same year. Following the two short-lived reigns of Güyük, Ogadai's son (1246–1248) and Möngke (1251–1259), the reins of command were passed on to Hulagu, Genghis Khan's grandson. It was he who led the Mongol troops into Mesopotamia and destroyed Baghdad in 1258 (as mentioned previously). Within eighteen days, the prestigious capital of the Muslim world was completely sacked and its cultural riches laid waste. Other prominent cities in Syria and the Fertile Crescent, such as Antioch and Tripoli, renowned for its prestigious library, met similar sad ends. Hulagu then reached the gates of Egypt but was defeated in 1260, by Mamluk sultan Qutuz, at the battle of Ain Jalut in Palestine. The Mamluks then drove the Mongols out of Syria and Palestine. The Mongol Empire was settled on the borders of the Zagros, separating Iran from Mesopotamia. The Mongols ultimately left the entire region in utter ruin, save Egypt. Indeed, the Syro-Mesopotamian ensemble was irreversibly shattered by its successive invasion by the Crusaders and the Mongols.

The Mongols entered history not only for their military feats, but also for the religious freedom that characterized their empire. Despite the horrors of the invasions, equality of cults became the order of the day across all conquered and pacified territories and the sovereigns were assisted by counsellors from all major religions without discrimination. The Nestorian Christians of Iran and the Far East as well as the Buddhists were highly influential in the court of the Mongol sovereigns. Thus, in central Asia and Iran, Islam lost – for some time – the leading position it had gained under the Arabs, Turks, and Iranians. In conquered territories, stretching from the Mediterranean to the Pacific, the 'Mongol peace' was the last episode of syncretism and religious tolerance in the Middle Ages.[10] Yet this 'golden

---

[10] See Chantal Lermercier-Quelquejay, *La Paix mongole. Joug tatar ou paix mongole?* (Paris: Flammarion, 1970); also René Grousset, *L'Empire mongol* (Paris: Payot, 1941).

age', which was coupled with a remarkable economic boost, was short-lived.

In 1295, Il-Khan Ghazan embraced Islam. Upon the death of his nephew, Abu Said in 1335, Mongol power ebbed in the Middle East. About a century later, a descendant of the Mongol dynasty, Tamerlane (Timurlenk, 1336–1405), resumed the expeditions with help from the Turkish tribes. Tamerlane was the founder of the Mughal Empire in the Indies (1526–1858), which was a synthesis of Indian and Islamic civilizations. Henceforth, the torch of Islamic civilization was permanently passed on to the Turks and Iranians, while the contributions of the Arabs became only marginal.

The history of the Iranian empires

The first eminent empire that can be labelled 'Persian' is that of the Medes in the 7th century BC, which was prolonged for another century in the domination of the great sovereigns of the Achaemenid Dynasty. The empire then stretched from the Indus Basin to the Mediterranean, covering all of Asia Minor, Thrace, the Mesopotamian Basin, Syria, and Egypt, which was conquered by Cambyses in 525 BC. It was Cyrus II who established Persian grandeur in the 6th century BC; Darius (522–486 BC) consolidated the empire and made Susa (Chaldea) its administrative capital and Persepolis its spiritual one. Despite the Assyrian violence, Cyrus was to go down in the annals of history for his liberal rule in conquered territories. Under Xerxes, the conquest of Greece failed after the naval defeat at Salamis (480 BC), which followed the earlier defeat of Darius at Marathon (490 BC); the Persian Empire thus failed in its conquest of the Mediterranean. It crumbled into 'satrapies' (provinces), virtually independent from central power, before falling into the hands of the Greeks with Alexander's conquests.

Stemming from the Kingdom of Parthia (250 BC to 226 CE), the second Persian Empire was made up of a population of Iranians and Scythians, and was founded on the shores of the Caspian Sea in the middle of the 3rd century BC. Confined to the Iranian high plateaus, this kingdom consolidated Zoroastrianism and paved the way for the rise of the eminent Sasanid Empire (3rd–7th centuries CE), which persisted until the Arab conquest and actively fought the expansion of Roman and Byzantine power in the Middle East.

Under the Sasanids, the Iranian centre of power was re-established in Mesopotamia, only sporadically reaching the Mediterranean shoreline. Though it was excluded from Anatolia, it still dominated all of Armenia and Azerbaijan, as well as the upper and lower Mesopotamian valley for several centuries. The capital of the empire, Ctesiphon, was located on the banks of the Tigris River, where ancient Neobabylonian capitals once rose. Ctesiphon, together with other capitals such as Constantinople and Alexandria in Egypt, was one of the greatest centres of civilization of the first centuries following the birth of Christ. The strong influence of the Zoroastrian religion and clergy upon the administration of imperial power constituted an efficient barrier to the dissemination of Christianity in that area of the Middle East. Nonetheless, 'heretical' Christian cults were acknowledged and accepted within the borders of the Empire: Monophysitism prevailed in Armenia and Nestorianism in Mesopotamia (where it is still practised to the present day). It was also under Shapur I in the 3rd century that Mani undertook his religious preaching, having an enduring impact, through the development of Gnostic beliefs, on the three monotheisms as well as on Hinduism.

The power held by the former Zoroastrian clergies, inherited from the ancient political and religious structures of the Babylonian and Assyrian empires, survives to the present day in the considerable political influence of the Shiite clergy in Islam. Indeed, it was Iran that provided Shiism, which was originally Arab, with a solid foothold with the Safavid Dynasty (see below). Shiism prevailed in the Muslim Middle East during the decline of the Abbasids and the expansion of the Ismailites of Cairo (10th to 11th centuries), under the Fatimid sovereigns, but it shrivelled up considerably under Turkish rule. Indeed, the Turks asserted their legitimacy by reinstating Sunnism and by setting the definitive version of the Islamic doctrines and jurisprudences, thus putting an end to the exceptional flowering of philosophy schools and of heterodox sects with manifest syncretistic tendencies that had characterized Islam in the first centuries of its existence. Nevertheless, Shiism and the main religious sects managed to survive by seeking shelter in mountainous areas where they could prosper away from central power's watchful eye. The Druzes of Lebanon and Syria, the Alawites of Syria and Turkey, the Ismailis all over central Asia and Asia Minor, the Yazidis of Iraq and Syria, are but few examples of such continued existence.

Contrary to the prevalent vision of Islam as a monolithic creed, Islam proved no less prone to disintegration than its Jewish and Christian predecessors, and crumbled into several clashing theologies and cults. Having sprung from the Orient, the monotheistic creeds could not escape the disguised influence of pagan pluralism. This pluralism, we believe, is but the manifestation of the tribal and ethnic specificities that define human societies. The ancient pagan cults and the religions of the Far East, based on ethics and individual fulfilment, allowed ethnic variety to perpetuate without any lasting politico-religious tragedies. And this is precisely what allowed pagan empires to grow stronger and to endure longer in the Middle East.

Shiism survived Turkish domination through the influence of certain Iranian-born dynasties such as the Tahirids and the Buyids, as well as through the expansion of Ismailism via the brilliant civilization of the Fatimid Dynasty of Egypt. Established in 1501 by Shah Ismail, the Safavid Dynasty stemmed from Sunni Turkmen tribes and was influenced by the mystical order founded by Sheikh Safi al-Din (hence the name Safavid). The Safavids gradually instituted Shiism as the official creed of the new realm. They rebuilt a vast Iranian state which expanded into Azerbaijan, the Caucasus, and central Asia, but also as far as Afghanistan and the Indies, not counting their numerous military campaigns to reconquer Mesopotamia, which had become Ottoman in the 16th century.

In reality, Iranian renaissance after the Arab conquest finally came to fruition at the dawn of the 9th century. It manifested in the revival of Persian, which had been eclipsed by the adoption of Arabic, the language of Koranic prophecy and the idiom of culture and science, in particular during the first two centuries of the Abbasid caliphate. After the decline of this empire, the Iranian dynasties, such as the Samanids (873–999), and the Turkish yet culturally Iranianized dynasties, such as the Ghaznavids (999–1030), developed considerably and established important centres of cultural enlightenment at Bukhara and Samarqand. This era also witnessed the flowering of Persian poetry with poets such as Daqiqi (935–980), Firdusi (932–1000), Omar Khayyam (1048–1131), Saadi (1213–1292), and Hafiz (1326–1390). The same applies to Persian philosophy with the illustrious Ibn Sina (980–1037), also know as Avicenna in the Western world, although most of his work was written in Arabic. Arabic declined progressively and became only used by non-Arab Muslim peoples in their religious studies. Persian, adopting the Arabic script, thus became the language of high culture in the Middle East, and even across central Asia and Muslim India.

Under the rule of Shah Abbas I, the capital of the Iranian kingdom was established in 1598 at Isfahan, where numerous architectural splendours were erected. However, the history of the new kingdom was characterized by a succession of relentless wars aiming to subdue the rebellious tribes and provinces, to resist the Ottoman invasions, and to extend borders. The ferocious struggles between the Ottomans and the Safavids for mastery of the Middle East ultimately exhausted both empires and turned them into easy targets for the increasingly voracious expansionist ambitions of Europe and Russia.

Following a period of decadence and disintegration of power (1747–1779), Aqa Mohammed Khan, the leader of the Turkmen Qajar tribe, reunified the empire and founded a new dynasty. The capital was thus transferred to Tehran in 1795. Politically, Persia remained enfeebled and unable to counter the inexorable rise of Russia in the Caucasus and central Asia, and the expansion of Great Britain, the leading colonial power in the Middle East and the Indies. In 1925, the last Qajar King was dethroned amid pressures and reformist demands from Iran's urban bourgeoisies; the reign of the Pahlavi Dynasty followed and ended in 1979, when the Shiite clergy seized power with Western consent.

Egypt and the Middle East

Egypt's history in the Middle East is more associated with its civilization and its influence than its military conquests. The Nile Valley was reunified and acquired political unity under the Pharaohs of the Ancient Empire at the end of the 4th millennium BC, and became a self-sufficient political entity. The borders of Egypt were set at that time and have remained the same ever since. This is the fundamental difference that distinguishes Egypt from the rest of the Middle East, and which has allowed it to exert a lasting influence on the entire region despite the vicissitudes of its history. The influence of Egyptian arts and commerce began to be felt in Mediterranean coastal regions and in Phoenician cities as early as the 4th millennium BC.

Following a period of decline due to the invasions of the Hyksos, a nomadic people of unknown origin, the New Empire (1590–1085 BC) fortified its defences considerably and marched on Asia Minor reaching the Euphrates. In the 13th century BC, the Egyptians and the Hittites joined forces against Assyria's rising power. Yet Egypt suffered a new eclipse as of the 12th century BC after its invasion by the Indo-European peoples known as 'the Sea Peoples' (whose feats in Greece and Asia Minor have been covered previously). Egyptian civilization remained brilliant and prosperous, including in the Lower Empire (1085–333), but the Egyptian armies were to remain confined to the Nile Valley until many centuries later, under the Fatimid and Ayyubid Muslim sovereigns.

Caught between Assyrian and Neo-Babylonian power, Egypt was invaded and occupied by the Assyrian armies in 663 BC; under the Saite Dynasty, Egypt established close ties with Greece. In turn, the interactions between those two cultures grew intense, thus setting the stage for Greek rule in the Middle East. Egypt became a safe haven particularly for the Jewish peoples who had been massively deported by Nebuchadnezzar upon his conquest of Palestine.

In 525 BC, Egypt fell into the hands of the Persian Achaemenid Empire and remained occupied until the arrival of the troops of Alexander the Great, who were welcomed by the Egyptians with a great sense of relief. Under the Ptolemy Dynasty, Hellenistic Egypt became a foremost cultural centre in the Middle East and the Mediterranean region. Egypt's conquest by the Romans under Cleopatra, and its subsequent colonization by the Byzantines, turned it into one of the most active centres of Middle Eastern Christianity, alongside Syria and Turkey. In those regions, monastic and anachoretic life flourished, particularly in desert areas such as the Sinai, or semi-desert ones such as the Orontes valley, lying on the Syro-Lebanese border, and Cappadocia, located on the Syro-Turkish borders. Saint Anthony, Saint Mark, Saint Maron, Saint Gregory, Saint Cyril, Saint Ephrem, and Saint John of Damascus are but a few of those who consolidated Christendom through their intellectual works and their exemplary existences.

After five centuries of Romano-Byzantine domination, in 637 CE Egypt was subjugated by the Arabs, who nevertheless chose Damascus and later Baghdad as their caliphate seats, rather than one of the great Pharaonic cities. Starting in the mid-9th century, the Turkish governors appointed by the Abbasid caliphate acted so as to enable Egypt to recover its political independence; these prefects founded local dynasties such as the Tulunids and the Ikhshidids. Intense Shia propaganda in its Northern African Ismaili form later endowed Egypt with a dynasty that was to restore its regional prestige. In 969, the Fatimids founded the city of Cairo, near ancient Memphis, the capital of the Ancient Empire, and created Al-Azhar University, which is still one of the foremost religious authorities in the Islamic world. The Fatimids then dominated Syria and Palestine. As of the mid-12th century, the Fatimid regime began to decline, until Saladin, vizier of Kurdish descent to the last Fatimid Caliph and the founder of the Ayyubid Dynasty, assumed power and consolidated his rule through his victories against the Franks. Nevertheless, Ayyubid power collapsed with the Crusaders' counter-attacks on Egypt (1249), which favoured the rise to power of the Mamluks, slave officers of Turkish descent, who commanded the Ayyubid army. The latter governed Egypt, Palestine, Syria, and Lebanon until the arrival of the Ottomans.

The Mamluks overthrew the last Latin kingdoms in the region and structured the resistance against the Mongols, who were defeated at Ain Jalut in Palestine (1260) – as discussed above – and were bound to relinquish all conquered territories. The Crusaders and the Mongols had disappeared from the Middle East by the close of the 13th century, as the region had fallen under the Seljuq Turks in Anatolia and Mesopotamia, and the Mamluks in Egypt, Syria, and Palestine. In 1517, the Ottomans occupied Cairo and permanently supplanted the Seljuq and Byzantine empires. Egypt was reborn politically three centuries later with the invasion of Napoleon Bonaparte in 1798. By weakening the Mamluks in Egypt, the French expedition allowed Muhammad Ali, a military officer of Albanian descent, to take over the country (1810) and to be acknowledged as viceroy in 1840 by the European powers. But for that, he was forced to abandon all his expansionist ambitions and his hopes of controlling the Arab provinces of the Ottoman Empire.

In 1830, Muhammad Ali had sent his armies into Syria, Palestine, and Lebanon, under the command of his son Ibrahim Pasha, in the hope of reaching Istanbul in order to oust the Ottoman Dynasty. This was the very last military conquest carried out by a Middle Eastern power in an attempt to restore the East–West balance of power. However, Muhammad Ali was stopped by the European powers. His fleet was destroyed and his wider conquest aims frustrated. In exchange, he was granted absolute control over Egypt and the right to found a dynasty. Although his successors pursued his modernizing efforts, they also dragged Egypt into crippling indebtedness vis-à-vis the European countries. Thus, Egyptian finances were placed under European trusteeship until the country came under British occupation in 1882.

PART II
THE MODERN MIDDLE EAST

4

THE FALL OF EMPIRES AND THE RISE OF WESTERN POWERS

Decadence of the East, renaissance of the West

There exists a striking contrast between the rise to power of the European states since the Renaissance and the progressive demise of the societies of the Middle East since the 18th century. The root causes of the decadence that befell the Middle East's great imperial structures – a topic of infinite controversy – will be discussed in more detail in Part III. It is worth noting, however, that the circumstances which led to the European Renaissance and to the Industrial Revolution in Europe are no less mysterious than the ones which led to decadence and decay on the other side of the Mediterranean. It may seem very tempting to compare the supposed genius of the West to the alleged fanaticism of the East, and walk the path of such eminent thinkers as Ernest Renan (1823–1892), who contrasted the 'heaviness' of the Semitic mind, embodied in Islam, with the 'genius' of Christian and Aryan Europe.

Yet only a multi-causal analysis can give a better understanding of such complex phenomena of decadence and renaissance which took place in the span of barely two centuries (the 17th and 18th centuries). Most historians agree that the standard of living and the level of scientific and technological knowledge were roughly similar on either side of the Mediterranean until the mid-18th century; that was before the Industrial Revolution spread throughout Europe and before the French Revolution and the Napoleonic conquests led to the emergence of all-powerful European nations.

In Europe, the seeds of the coming to power of this small-sized continent could no doubt be found in an array of fields (cultural, economical, social, and technological); some were even sown as far back as the Middle Ages with the first European theologians who had heralded the secularization of thought. Moreover, Europe also greatly benefited from the Spanish and Portuguese naval expeditions to the Far East and the Americas, which brought new precious metals and cultures into the continent. Thereafter, Europe broke out of its shell and discovered the great Persian, Indian, and Chinese civilizations. This aroused an unending curiosity which was to achieve its sharpest formulation in the arts, literature, philosophy, and science.

In the Orient, the great imperial structures were at the peak of their power and territorial expansion in the 17th century; there was nothing to signal that the small European political entities, compared with the vastness of the Middle Eastern empires, were already on the path of ever-accelerating progress. Although Europe had been weakened by its previous wars of religion, thereafter, apart from the Napoleonic wars and later the Franco-German war of 1870, the continent was to enjoy an enduring stability; the borders of the nascent nation-states were gradually fixed, and no external force came to threaten European territory.

The Middle East went the opposite way. The incessant wars, invasions and counter-invasions that raged for over two centuries (16th and 17th) in the Caucasian region, Mesopotamia, the Anatolian plateau, and Central Asia, eventually exhausted the Safavids and the Ottomans. And yet, both empires continued to pursue their ambitions of expansion into the Indian continent and Asia Minor, and even into Europe in the case of the Ottoman Empire. Under such conditions, it was not surprising to see those two empires decline and their populations dwindle. This aroused the lust of France, Britain, Tsarist Russia, and the Habsburg Empire, and eased the path for the progressive dismemberment of the Ottoman and Iranian realms.

As Europe progressed and bloomed, the Middle East fell into a steadily worsening state of decay. Despite the tardy efforts of modernization exerted in both the Ottoman Empire and the Persian monarchy, the gap between them and Europe kept growing wider. In time, Europe progressively subjugated the whole region, as far as the Indies and the Far East; and the Middle East was soon compelled to march to the European beat. This meant embracing a different culture, modernizing its structures, and withstanding the military, economic, and cultural invasion of the great European powers, utterly powerless in the face of this growing domination. As previously mentioned, as soon as European domination subsided, the United States, in direct alliance with the State of Israel, took the relay and deployed its arsenal in the heart of the Arab world as of 1990.

Thus, not surprisingly, the Middle East remained a region of tempests and instabilities, of revolts and mutinies, taking the most diverse ideological and religious colours and using the most unexpected of weapons: plane hijackings, hostage situations, suicide commando missions and terrorism in all its forms, whether abroad or within the local political struggles.

A deeply de-structuring conquest

One might be tempted to situate the end of Antiquity in the Middle East at the close of the 18th century, or rather in 1919, at the end of the First World War. But it is indeed the irruption of the European and later American powers, from Napoleon Bonaparte to the present day, which definitively broke the Middle East's political structures – inherited from an almost uninterrupted succession of empires with centres in Mesopotamia, the high Iranian plateau, Macedonia, Thrace, Anatolia, and the Nile Valley.

From Napoleon Bonaparte in 1798, to the landing of U.S. troops in the Arabian peninsula in 1990, including the British and French occupations of Egypt, Mesopotamia, Syria, and Lebanon, and then the conquest of Palestine in 1948 by the Jewish survivors of the European anti-Semitic persecutions, all such events signal a profound rupture in the history of the Middle East. As of then, it was to be modelled and dictated by the Europeans, the Israelis, and the Americans. Apart from the short interlude of the Cold War – during which U.S.–Soviet competition gave the newly de-colonized states a certain margin of independence on the international scene – the modern Middle East remained an object of both fear and desire to the West. But unlike the ancient Greeks and even the Romans, who shared similar cultural structures and comparable levels of technical knowledge with the main peoples of the Middle East, the Europeans – notably the Ashkenazi Jewish colonists fleeing anti-Semitic persecution – and the Americans who invaded and installed themselves in the Middle East, had their own historical and cultural background; and theirs was a completely different experience of the previous few centuries from that of the local populations.

The European powers did not regard the conquest of the Middle East as a goal per se, with the sole purpose of achieving a new superior synthesis of civilization, as had been the case with all the previous conquerors, in particular the Greeks, Persians, Arabs, and Turks. Rather, it was almost exclusively motivated by the rivalries between the European powers and the strategic and economic advantages the

Middle East had to offer. This was the case in the 19th century, when the two greatest European empires, France and Britain, violently locked horns in the Middle East over the control of the road to India – which had previously led to Napoleon Bonaparte's expedition in Egypt. The discovery of enormous reserves of oil in the region during the 20th century triggered dire rivalries and fierce colonial squabbles between the French and the British, as each wanted a share of this much-coveted region. Just like Egypt and Mesopotamia had been the granaries of the Roman Empire, the Middle East was to become an indispensable reservoir of energy resources (oil and gas) from which Europe and later the United States drew strength in order to assert their domination.

In the mid-20th century, the Western decision-makers were mainly concerned with the consolidation of the new State of Israel (created in 1947–1948) and the protection of its new territorial conquests in the West Bank in the aftermath of the Arab–Israeli war in 1967. But by serving those goals, the Westerners overturned the region's millennial socio-political structures and unleashed acute internal tensions in the heart of the local societies. Such tensions were to become the source of terrorist movements inspired by an array of Islamic militant ideologies that supplanted the Arab, Turkish, and Iranian nationalisms, of secular and sometimes socialist tinctures, which had prevailed for over a century (1850–1979). Initially, such movements, detailed subsequently, were actually encouraged by the West to fight the expansion of Marxist ideology and Soviet influence in the Middle East.[11]

---

[11] See Georges Corm, *Le Proche-Orient éclaté...*, op. cit., pp. 803–853.

The three main models of resistance to European domination

Three models of resistance to European domination can be identified in the Middle East – the Turkish, the Iranian and the Arab – each owing its birth to a specific set of historical conditions. The Arab model, which came last historically, was highly influenced by the Turkish and Iranian forms which preceded it.

The Turkish model was fashioned by the secular and nationalistic ideology of the Young Turks officers towards the end of the 19th century, but also by Kemalism – so called after General Mustapha Kemal Pasha, or Atatürk (1881–1938), who successfully founded modern Turkey, now geographically limited to Anatolia. This model was deeply influenced by the ideology of the French Revolution and by the Jacobin concept of a compact and homogenous nation-state, but also by the ethnic and linguistic nationalism that arose in Germany. It was based on the rejection of religious-based power and on a fierce nationalist ideology, 'Turanism' or the cult of Turkish ethnic origin, which was made the prime criterion of the nation.[12] This model favoured the homogenization of the peoples of the Anatolian plateau by expulsing and exchanging populations with Greece; the peoples of Hellenistic origin that had been living in Anatolia for centuries were traded for Turkic-speaking ones living in Greece. The great mass of Armenians suffered an even more sordid fate, being either massacred in reprisal for their

---

[12] See Étienne Copeaux, *Espace et temps de la nation turque. Analyse d'une historiographie nationaliste 1931–1993* (Paris: Éditions du CNRS, 1997); and also *Bernard Lewis, Islam et Laïcité. La naissance de la Turquie moderne* (Paris: Fayard, 1988).

Western-sponsored revolt or expulsed to Soviet Armenia. Be that as it may, this model gave Turkey a solid stability and made it a regional power to be reckoned with; one fostering good relations with Western countries, without however being reduced to a docile pawn.

In the last decades of the 20th century, admiration for Kemalism waned due to several concurrent factors: the inexorable rise of diverse forms of Islamic fundamentalism in the Middle East (elaborated subsequently); the influence of European liberal democracy over Turkey, which facilitated the acceptance of the rise of religious and ethnic identitarian movements to the detriment of the Jacobin and secular definitions of the state; and finally, also due to the same European influence, the weariness of Turkish public opinion towards the interventions of the military in public life carried out in the name of the strict secularism of the state. All such factors explain the success of the moderate Islamic party in ruling the country since 2003 without any major incidents, after having acquired an absolute majority in the parliament at the end of the previous year (as we shall see, a first attempt at forming a government had failed in 1996–1997).

The Iranian model is not unreminiscent of its Turkish peer. Indeed, both aspired to modernize their respective countries and both introduced modern political institutions, exemplified by the adoption of Parliamentarism as of 1908. This model was also deeply marked by European-style nationalism. Nonetheless, due to the absence of a leading figure with undisputed authority such as Mustapha Kemal in Turkey, the Iranian model received many different and contradictory influences which pervaded the various elements of Iranian society – now confronted with the double rise of Russo-British hegemony over the affairs of the monarchy.[13] This model was also characterized by a paradoxical blend of conservatism and progressivism in the clergy, as well as by anti-imperialism and social revolts clashing with the interests of both the royal court and the affluent landowners. This mixture exploded into a very troubled and violent period which led to the Islamic Revolution in 1979.

This latter sought to merge all opposing intellectual currents into the astonishing *Velayat Faqih* political theory (control by religious jurists), whereby a religious guide, assisted by a council, oversees and controls the functioning of the executive, parliament and judiciary, with respect to their compliance with Islamic Shiite jurisprudence. This system is a peculiar mix of constitutionalism, inspired by the West, and of authoritarianism, acquired by the most conservative faction of the religious class through the convulsions of the revolution, and the elimination of its secular, bourgeois and liberal, or populist and socialist components, as well as of the prestigious religious figures who opposed the *Velayat Faqih* system and regarded it as alien to the Shiite jurisprudential traditions.[14]

Finally, next to these two models, we must mention the Egyptian Nasserist model of revolution and nationalist military dictatorship, which was somewhat inspired by the Kemalist model. Gamal Abdel Nasser was the strongest man in the Arab world and the Middle East from 1956 to 1970, and an immensely popular figure in the whole of the region. The

---

[13] On this topic, see Vanessa Martin, *Islam and Modernism. The Iranian Revolution of 1906* (London: I.B. Tauris, 1989).

[14] Regarding the confiscation of the revolution by the conservative wing of the Shiite religious dignitaries, led by the Imam Khomeini, see the book of the former president of the Republic of Iran who was forced to flee the country during his term: Abol Hassan Sadr, *Le Complot des ayatollahs* (Paris: La Découverte, 1989).

political and economical transformations in Egypt inspired a number of other countries. The Arab model also drew on the Yugoslav experiment with communism, due to the close relations between Egypt and Yugoslavia during the era of Third World countries' 'Positive Neutrality'. It was characterized by the political elimination of the vast class of feudal landowners and the rich bourgeoisie, which held close ties with Western societies; by the one-party ideological dictatorship; and by a massive wave of nationalizations that struck the interests of the major Western companies, then those of the leading local capitalists.[15] This model spread like wildfire into the region, mainly in Syria, Iraq, Libya, and the Sudan. It preached ideological anti-imperialism, hostility toward Israel with the aim of granting the Palestinians the rights of self-determination and return (for those who were forced to leave the territories occupied by Israel), and Pan-Arab nationalism, which was supposed to lead to the abolishment of the artificial state borders defined by the French and British colonial masters after the fall of the Ottoman Empire in 1919.

Yet, Nasser's defeat to Israel in 1967, then his premature death in 1970, led to a considerable decline of the Arab nationalist doctrines of secular nature. However, this vacuum was rapidly filled by the fulgurant rise of diverse forms of conservative – even fundamentalist – Islam imported from Saudi Arabia, in the specific framework of the Cold War and the sudden enrichment of the oil-exporting states of the Arabian peninsula. Thus, Arab nationalism was eclipsed by the 'Islamic revival' (*Sahwa*), a movement relentlessly promoted by Saudi Arabia and many Arab countries of the Arabian peninsula, not only in the

---

[15] See the work of Jean and Simone Lacouture, *L'Égypte en mouvement* (Paris: Seuil, 1962); and also Jean Lacouture, *Nasser* (Paris: Seuil, 1971).

Arab world but also in Turkey, Africa, Indonesia and wherever Muslim communities could be found. This Islamic 'revival' was translated into the 're-Islamicization' of society in many an aspect (the creation of Islamic banks, the increase of religious shows in the media, a strict observance of religious rites, such as the fast and pilgrimage, social pressure on women to wear the veil, the making of Islamic mobile phones providing prayer hours and dolls dressed the Islamic way, etc).[16] This re-Islamicization was intensified when U.S. troops disembarked in the Arabian peninsula in 1990 to liberate Kuwait from Iraqi occupation, then invaded Iraq in 2003 from the permanent American military bases in this region of the Middle East.

Under European and later American sway, the Middle East underwent four distinctive periods, which we will now examine successively below.

---

[16] For further details, see Georges Corm, *La Question religieuse au XXIe siècle. Géopolitique et crise de la postmodernité* (Paris: La Découverte, 2006), pp. 145–160; and also *Le Proche-Orient éclaté...*, op. cit., pp. 803–853.

5

THE MIDDLE EAST UNDER EUROPEAN DOMINATION

European rivalries and new territorial partitions (1798–1918)

Europe's rise to power and its impact on the Middle East

As previously seen, the Arab, Greek, Iranian, and Egyptian domains were incorporated into the Turkish military and administrative orbit. Turkish power under the Ottomans had threatened the whole of Europe by twice laying siege to Vienna; it was also deeply rooted in Eastern Europe, more specifically in the Balkans. The European nations began to assert their power from the 16th century onwards, with the Renaissance of arts and literature, the Age of Enlightenment, and the Industrial Revolution, until European power finally encircled and then suffocated the vast Ottoman realms. But it was no doubt Europe's naval ascendancy that ushered the demise of the Ottoman Empire, symbolized in the victory of the coalition of European fleets over the Ottomans at Lepanto (1571). Owing to this naval upper hand, the Portuguese and the Spanish, followed by the British and the French, were able to colonize America, to reach and circumnavigate the African coasts, and to create the first trade posts in the Indies. Consequently, the Middle Eastern empires, lying at the age-old intersection between the three continents of Europe, Asia, and Africa, ceased to benefit from the intense commercial traffic they had hitherto enjoyed. Thus deprived of its naval power, the Ottoman Empire saw all its possessions threatened by the rise to power of the European states and empires.

With the Industrial Revolution, Europe improved its military techniques and organizational skills, which sealed its ascendancy over the Ottomans despite the Empire's many efforts from the 18th century to reform its civil and military administration. The Napoleonic wars also contributed to develop the mobility of the European armies over very long distances, a manoeuvre quasi-monopolized by the Turkish armies ever since the 13th century and the defeat of the Crusades. But the European powers pursued contradictory ambitions which allowed the Ottoman Empire to survive longer than otherwise would have been possible. This indeed prolonged the existence of the Ottoman political entity, but only artificially, despite its natural legitimacy as heir of all the great Middle Eastern empires. The economic and social structures of the Middle East were too archaic to keep pace with the new trends in international trade and balance of political power endorsed by the European states since the discovery of the Americas. Thereafter, European power drew its strength from the thriving Atlantic economy, engendered by the colonization of the American continent. In sum, Europe was no longer a limited and fragile space cornered by the empires of the Middle East, as had been the case during the Persian, Arab, and Turkish invasions, but a formidable power with a solid foothold in the Atlantic region and the Americas and a monopoly over all their riches and their economic promise.

It was also the infiltration of European ideas that eroded the legitimacy of the imperial structures of the Middle East; in particular those of the French Revolution had a tremendous impact on numerous elites. Concepts such as equality, fraternity, and justice were indeed deeply rooted in this part of the world, whereas the practice of despotism in the many empires of the region had only one plausible justification: the need to secure the territory against invasions and chaos. Indeed, despotism had always borne a shocking aspect, since religion preached love and tolerance, but also, with Christianity and Islam, the equality of all believers before a single God. Thus, the European ideas were to rekindle the dormant flames of resentment against despotic rule. The Arabs, the Persians, and the Turks who travelled to the great European capitals in the 19th and 20th centuries found active representative regimes of democracy, even in kingdoms, saw the role of women in literature and arts, even in politics, and modern educational and industrial systems. In Persia, as in the Ottoman Empire, this resulted in acute tensions between the government and the urban elites, which further undermined the fragile political systems in place.

It is unfortunately the brutal forms of European colonialism and its contempt toward its own democratic principles in its interventions in the Middle East that have constituted – and still do – a powerful obstacle to the dissemination of democratic principles in this region of the world. Over the last two centuries, the values of individual democracy have flowed and ebbed in the region according to the nature of the European interventions, followed by those of the Israelis and Americans, whose excesses have favoured the rise of movements of rejection and of identitarian self-confinement, falling back on the so-called traditionalist values to the detriment of the former liberal and modernizing movements. It must be added that the strong influence of Tsarist Russia, and later of the Soviet Union, on the Middle East has also adversely affected the development of democratic 'bourgeois' and liberal tendencies.

European nationalist ideas also travelled to the Balkans and to Anatolian and Mesopotamian Asia Minor, where they had an equally negative impact. The populations in those areas, a mosaic of different ethnic origins with a multiplicity of religions, had always lived together side by side, often mixing despite their differences, under the arbitration of imperial rulers. But the games of influence played by the European powers and then the disappearance of these imperial masters led to numerous tragedies, massacres, and transfers of populations: the two recent crises of Lebanon (1975–1990) and the disintegration of Yugoslavia (1992–1995), but also the Iraqi convulsions triggered by the American invasion of Mesopotamia, were but a repetition of similar events which were to mark the whole history of the Ottoman collapse.[17]

The main stages of political reform and the dismemberment of the Ottoman Empire

In the first half of the 19th century, seeking to assert their dominance but not yet to dismember the Empire, the European powers sought to create territorial nationalisms over which they could exert a direct political influence, through the local communities, whether religious (Maronites in Lebanon, Nestorian Chaldeans in Iraq and Persia, Druzes in Lebanon, Alawites in Syria, Copts in Egypt, and Catholics in Albania, etc.) or ethnic (Armenians, Greeks, Slavs, Orthodox Albanians, Azerbaijanis, and Kurds) that were still under Ottoman or sometimes Persian rule.

The dismemberment of the Empire started when the French gave their support to Muhammad Ali in Egypt – who, as previously seen, overthrew the Mamluks after the retreat of

---

[17] For this topic, see Georges Corm, *L'Europe et l'Orient. De la balkanisation à la libanisation, histoire d'une modernité inaccomplie* (Paris: La Découverte, 1989).

the French armies, then occupied Syria, Palestine, and Lebanon in 1831, and even threatened Istanbul. He decreed equality between Muslims and non-Muslims in all his conquered territories. But under pressure from the British, whose fleets savagely bombarded Beirut in 1840 to force him to evacuate Lebanon and Syria, and also the Russians and the Austrians, Muhammad Ali returned to Egypt where he was recognized as viceroy by the European powers. But the Egyptian economy was reeling under the weight of its accumulated debts between 1840 and 1870 vis-à-vis the European financial markets, which led to Egypt being placed under economic and political trusteeship. This triggered a nationalist uprising in 1879, which served the British as a pretext to occupy Egypt in 1882 and to imprison Urabi, a military officer who dared defy European hegemony. But it was not until the definitive dethroning of the Egyptian monarchy in 1952 in a military coup, with the benevolent support of the United States, that Egypt was finally able to shake off the English yoke.

Just like the French had driven Egypt to claim autonomy from the Ottomans, which eventually brought it under British dominion, the Russians, although halted by the British, encouraged the Greeks to rebel against the Empire. In spite of the important role played by the Greeks in the administration of the Balkan provinces of the Ottoman Empire, the prominence of the Patriarchate of Istanbul, whose leader was the second highest-ranking religious dignitary after Sheikh al-Islam (Islam's foremost legal authority), and the interests of the mercantile Greek bourgeoisie, a rebellion, originally starting in Romania in 1825 and demanding the modernization and the democratization of the Empire, broke out in earnest and resulted in the secession of Peloponnesus and Thessaly. This uprising was accompanied by an Albanian revolt. Such insurrections led to the emergence of a small Greek kingdom, which only comprised a fraction of the Greeks of the Empire and was endowed with a Bavarian king in 1832; later on, the British installed on the throne the youngest son of the King of Denmark, who reigned from 1863 to 1913. Between 1913 and 1920, the Greek territory grew progressively with the victories of the Balkan wars which forced the Empire to relinquish its European possessions gradually. This retreat was always accompanied by migratory waves of Turkish or Turkicized populations from the Balkans to Anatolia. Until 1947, Greece was to remain torn between the political and military influences of Russia and Britain, which kept the country in permanent instability.

Between 1840 and 1861, Lebanon was also torn by Anglo–French rivalries in the Mediterranean, the French pushing the Maronites to emancipate from Ottoman rule, and the British countering by supporting and arming an alliance of Druzes and Ottomans. The central part of the country thereby became a condominium of the European powers, which compelled the Ottomans to appoint a Christian Ottoman governor to administer Lebanese affairs.

As the dismemberment of the Ottoman Empire commenced, the European powers actively extolled the merits of democracy to the sultans of Istanbul. In 1839, the *Tanzimat* period was set in motion. A first important decree of reforms was adopted that year, and was confirmed and completed in 1856 by a second similar decree, then was crowned by the adoption of an Ottoman constitution in 1876 and the election of a short-lived parliament, which was quickly dissolved by the Sultan; it was not recalled until 1908 and was again suspended a few months later. The Empire also acquired a modern code of commerce (1850), a penal code (1858), a nationality code, and established the Council of State, as well as an assembly of provincial representatives from the different religious and ethnic communities of each province.

However, even the promulgation of a constitution by the sultan Abdel Hamid in 1876, under pressure from the reformist party of the 'Young Turks', was no longer enough to calm the restless masses, no more than the proclamation of a Persian constitution by the sovereign in 1906, amid pressures from the bourgeois elites, as we shall see. Russia was increasingly gaining ground: after taking Georgia, Dagestan, and the Armenian districts of Erevan and Nakhitchevan (1813–1828) from the Persian kingdom, the Russians won large parts of the Caucasus (1829) and the Crimea. But these new conquests triggered, between 1856 and 1858, a massive Anglo–French military response that was translated into a particularly deadly war to halt the ambitions of Tsarist Russia, whose military might now posed an imminent threat to Istanbul. The Russians, the French, and the British also armed the Armenians, in anticipation of the coming wars, which did not fail to erupt and to administer the coup de grâce to the dying empire, thus bringing its territories into the European orbit.

In parallel, throughout the 19th century, the British had extended their political and military influence across the coasts of the Arabian peninsula: Aden was occupied in 1889 and protection treaties were concluded with the tribal chiefs of the eastern coast of the peninsula, also called the Pirate Coast (the Trucial States). In the aftermath of the First World War, after the fall of the empires of Russia, Austro-Hungary, and Germany (a former ally of the Ottoman Empire), the entire Middle East lay open to the hegemonic ambitions of the French and the British, now left in sole control of this strategic region.

Iran under strong Russo-British influence

In Iran, the Russian and British influences became felt more heavily as of the 19th century. To modernize its economy and its civil and military institutions, the Persian monarchy, just like the dynasty of Muhammad Ali in Egypt and the Ottoman sultans, pleaded for European aid. Iran mainly obtained assistance from Britain and Russia, a powerful and threatening neighbour with which it fostered close relations, predominantly military as demonstrated by Russia's establishment of a Cossack Brigade to serve as a praetorian guard for the reigning family. The country's oil resources only made it more alluring to the European powers, but it was the British who succeeded in obtaining a quasi-monopoly not only over the Iranian oil concessions, but also over several other sectors including the state-owned tobacco companies. The Persian monarchy, like that of Egypt and the Ottoman sultanate, was constantly over-indebted vis-à-vis the European powers and its tax revenues were consequently pledged against European loans.

As in the Ottoman Empire, reforms, revolts, and foreign interventions multiplied. In 1906, a year of numerous anti-British revolts, the monarchy adopted a constitution and Iran saw its first elections. But the Shah, as well as the European powers and the conservative religious elements, quickly moved to paralyze this new institution which allowed the expression of modernist and nationalist tendencies. Public life degenerated quickly, and the reigning dynasty became increasingly discredited until it collapsed in 1925 and was replaced by the Pahlavi dynasty. But the difficulties that plagued the country quickly wore down the new monarchy as it became torn between the rival ambitions of the two powers sharing influence over Iran, Russia and Britain; this twin-rule was consecrated by the Russo-British Convention of Saint Petersburg in 1907.

In the 19th century, Persia became a sort of laboratory measuring the choc of modernity upon the different elites and social classes, including the clergy, itself deeply torn between modernists and backward-looking conservatives. It was amid this turmoil that the key figure of Sayyid Ali Mohammad (1819–1850) emerged, also known as 'Al-Bab' (the Door), who founded a new religion of a syncretistic and rationalistic nature that grew highly popular in Iran. But the success of the new religion prompted a violent reaction from the influential caste of Muslim clerics, which degenerated into riots and street fights and ended in the Bab being arrested, sentenced to death, and executed in Tabriz. His successor, Mirza Hussein Ali (1817–1892), escaped the violence and repression in Iran and settled in Palestine, where the doctrine of Babism became 'Bahaism' – whose followers are persecuted to this day in many Muslim countries, but more vehemently so in Iran since the Revolution of 1979.

Direct Anglo–French domination over the Arab world (1919–1956)

France and the United Kingdom certainly aimed for the definitive dismemberment of the Turco-Irano-Arab Middle East in its entirety and for the partitioning of the territories emerging from its dismemberment into small political entities placed under their domination. Throughout the First World War, many agreements and treaties were accordingly signed between them and Italy and Russia, including the famous Sykes-Picot treaty (May 1916) which defined the respective British and French spheres of influence in the Arab territories and set the stage for the Ottoman dismemberment. Moreover, in the declaration of the Foreign Office Secretary, Lord Arthur James Balfour (1917), the British government promised the establishment of a 'national home' for the Jewish communities of Europe in Palestine; yet at the same time the British promised the Sharif of Mecca, Husayn ibn Ali, assistance to create an Arab kingdom spreading over the Hijaz, the territories of the Fertile Crescent and Mesopotamia, in the event of an Arab insurrection against the Turks (Hussein-McMahon correspondence). This revolt effectively erupted in 1916 and the British government was confronted with its contradictory promises. The French had been promised control over the Syro-Lebanese littoral and northern Mesopotamia in the Sykes-Picot agreement; the Zionist Movement, a national Jewish home in Palestine; and the Arabs, a unified and independent large Arab kingdom comprising the Hijaz – governed by the Hashemites – and the other Arab provinces of the Ottoman Empire to the east of the Mediterranean (Lebanon, Syria, Palestine, and Iraq).

During the Paris Peace Conference, which was held to address post-war problems and was crowned by the signing of the Versailles Treaty in June 1919, the United States tried to counter the imperialistic ambitions of the two victorious European powers. The American government had indeed helped the Allies in their struggle against Germany, based on the principles of President Wilson calling for self-determination for all peoples, free of constraints, and for the creation of a 'League of Nations' consisting of free, sovereign, and equal states. An American investigation commission in the Middle East (the King Crane Commission) confirmed the ardent desire of the Arabs of the Fertile Crescent to unite within one state under the rule of the Hashemite family of Mecca; this commission warned against the brutal application of Zionist principles in Palestine, arguing that this would lead to the eviction of the Arab population and perpetual instability and wars; it also advised against the carving up of Turkish Anatolia between the Armenians, Italians, Greeks, and Kurds, which was indeed on the European agenda – as was later evidenced by the Treaty of Sevres (1921).

The Allies disregarded the American warnings, and the U.S. Senate refused to ratify the charter of the 'League of Nations' endorsing the Anglo–French views. Without American military assistance, however, the British and the French proved unable to tame the blazing flames of nationalism which consumed the Middle East, and were further fuelled by the empty and inconsistent promises made to the Arabs. Bolshevik propaganda also denounced the imperialist manoeuvres and secret diplomacies and called on the peoples of the East to rebel against the European powers. Under popular domestic pressure, the British and French governments were compelled to demobilize their troops. In 1915, the Armenians and the Kurds were the first to be jettisoned, in order that Britain and France's grip on their Arab possessions could be better maintained; as previously mentioned, this had disastrous consequences for the Armenians, who found themselves under double pressure from the Turkish army reconstituted under Atatürk and from armed bands of Kurds (another people that fell victim to the Allies' false promises). In 1922, the significant Greek populations of Asia Minor, particularly in Smyrna (ancient Pergamum), were also massacred after Greek troops, invited by the Allies to disembark on the Turkish Mediterranean coast, were crushed by Turkish counteroffensives.

In Syria, Faysal, a member of the Hashemite family, who had led the Arab revolt from 1916 to 1918 against the

Ottomans with British support, in particular that of Colonel
Lawrence, took residence in Damascus where a National
Congress of the people proclaimed him king in 1920. But
the French troops of General Henri Gouraud forced him to
abdicate his throne barely a year later. The French and the
British then concluded new arrangements. In exchange for a
share in Mosul's petroleum exploitation, France was to
relinquish all its territorial possessions in the Middle East,
except for Syria and Lebanon. King Faysal was expelled from
Damascus and transferred in 1921 to Baghdad, which
became the capital of modern-day Iraq; another member of
the Hashemite family, Abdullah, was appointed king in
Transjordan in 1924. The French thus consolidated their
domination over Lebanon and Syria. Lebanon was
proclaimed the State of Greater Lebanon (Etat du Grand
Liban) in 1920, by annexing the territories that had been
taken from it under a 1861 protocol, as well as the Syrian
port of Tripoli and its backcountry (the fertile plains of
Akkar). Syria, on the other hand, was divided into several
administrative states (Alawite, Druze, Sunnite in Damascus
and Aleppo, in addition to Alexandretta and the port of
Antioch, which was later ceded to the Turks in 1939 in
reward for their neutral stance during World War II).

The British firmly established their control over Iraq and
Palestine and completed discrediting the Hashemites by
placing the Saud family over the Hijaz and the holy places of
Mecca and Medina in 1924–1925, and by allowing it to
found the Kingdom of Saudi Arabia in 1932 by annexing to
the Hijaz the deserts of Najd and Rub' al Khali. However,
the old Saudi enterprise to found a large Bedouin empire
governed by a mythological return to the primitive sources
of Islam as taught in the mid-18th century by Muhammed
ibn Abd al-Wahhab, a preacher sponsored by the Sauds, was

to witness many vicissitudes. As early as 1811, the troops of Muhammad Ali of Egypt were sent off to stamp out this armed religious movement which was threatening to bring Syria and Mesopotamia under its sway. The Saudi efforts resumed again, albeit still in vain, towards the end of the 19th century, although this time the Wahhabi warriors were able to reach and sack Karbala, a Shiite holy site in Iraq. It was not until the colonial era that the Saudi enterprise finally succeeded and developed under the British and later American wings.[18]

Throughout the 'Mandates' era (French and British), all Arab aspirations of 'modernist' and democratic tendencies were systematically frustrated. The Arab territories of the Ottoman Empire had been broken down into several political or administrative autonomous entities governed by foreign non-Muslim armies: republics in Syria (gradually unified) and Lebanon, constitutional kingdoms in Transjordan, Iraq, and Egypt, and an Islamic kingdom in Saudi Arabia with a brutal and fundamentalist application of the *Shariah*. Moreover, the British and the French did not put into practice the very democratic principles they proclaimed elsewhere. Even though the countries that fell under their 'Mandate' were formally given a constitution and a parliament, the 'High Commissioners' (Hauts Commissaires) summarily suspended all constitutional life the moment nationalist protests and claims for independence began encroaching on the established colonial order.

In Palestine, the British were confronted with two conflicting agitations: that of the Jewish immigrants, whose

---

[18] On Wahhabism, see the key work of Henri Laoust, *Les Schismes dans l'islam* (Paris: Payot, 1965), which provides a panoramic view of Islam's different schools and interpretations.

numbers kept increasing with the escalation of anti-Semitism in Europe; and that of the Palestinians themselves, who were beginning to feel threatened by this mounting tide of Jewish immigrants. The immigrants were concentrating in their agricultural colonies, the Kibbutz, and were already organizing themselves under state-like structures. The struggle, put on hold by the Second World War, resumed with increased intensity in 1946, when some Jewish immigrants waged ravaging terrorist attacks against the British garrison and began to arm themselves openly in order to directly counter the Arab pressures and revolts. The British, no longer able to handle the situation they themselves had created, resorted to the newly formed United Nations (UN) which decided in 1947 to divide the territory between the Jews and the Palestinians, but recommended the internationalization of Jerusalem and the holy places.

War between the two communities was inevitable. The Palestinians, supported by the other Arab countries, opposed the decision of the United Nations. Thereafter, the Arab–Israeli conflict was to become a permanent fixture of the Middle Eastern political landscape with a succession of wars (1948, 1956, 1967 and 1973), the occupation of a large area of South Lebanon in 1978, then the invasion of half of Lebanon by the Israeli army in 1982, including its capital Beirut, and finally the war against Hezbollah during the summer of 2006. But the defeat of the Arab armies to the Jewish state in 1948 bore other consequences: it completely discredited the political regimes installed by France and Britain at the end of World War I and paved the way for an era of military coups, inter-Arab discords, and the rise of Islamic movements hostile to Western hegemony.

In Iran, the Pahlavi dynasty that succeeded the Qajars in 1925 began to wane in 1952–1953 when Mohammed

Mosaddeq, a prominent liberal bourgeois, became prime minister and nationalized, with wide popular support, the Iranian oil sector, which had hitherto been entirely controlled by Anglo-Saxon companies. The Shah went into exile in Italy and the internal situation went from bad to worse. The CIA orchestrated a coup against Mosaddeq, who was arrested; the more conservative elements of the religious caste supported the coup, thus allowing the Shah to return a few months after his exile. This direct American intervention in the interior affairs of Iran was to leave a lasting impact on Iranian opinion which set the stage for the revolution of 1979 and its virulent anti-American stance.

As with Iran, several combined factors account for the revolution that erupted in Egypt in 1952: the corruption of the monarchy; Western economic control over national resources; the interventions of the superpowers in internal affairs; the agitation of public opinion and the general social discontent. In both countries, opinion was deeply torn between communist, socialist, or liberal nationalists, and conservative or modernist religious elements, both anti-imperialist. This could explain the long struggle for power between the different factions, which stood united against the outside world but were extremely divided ideologically on the inside, hence the violence and the long periods of dictatorship that preceded the tempering of the revolution and the return to more open policies, mainly as regards the economy.

Only Turkey, under the energetic direction of Atatürk, was to effectively transform into a strong and relatively stable state. Mustapha Kemal, the founder of modern Turkey, unlike other Arab leaders, was the only Middle Eastern leader who was able to expel all occupying European troops (British, French, Greek, and Italian armies) from his territory. Owing to the prestige he thus acquired, he abolished the caliphate in 1923, established secularism and traded the Arabic alphabet in which Turkish had hitherto been written for a new Latin script. He thus turned his back on the Ottoman and Muslim past of Anatolia, with the firm intention of accelerating Turkey's modernization in line with the European model by homogenizing its population. He was to make of Turkey a key anti-Soviet rampart, since the USSR had resumed its former imperialistic policies in the Middle East and even begun to threaten Western hegemony.

6

THE MIDDLE EAST CAUGHT BETWEEN THE COLD WAR, OIL RESOURCES, AND THE ARAB–ISRAELI CONFLICT

U.S.–Soviet rivalries in the East

From 1945 until the collapse of the USSR in 1991–1992, the Western European states had mainly one concern: the rise of Soviet power in the Middle East. In the immediate aftermath of the war, the Western powers pursued many interests in the Middle East that they deemed highly strategic and vital for their own security. This region was indeed a crossroads in communications, essential to secure a fast deployment of their military troops into India and the Far East, where the USSR had gained considerable political ground through the triumph of communism in China and the development of communist parties in the whole of the Indochinese peninsula. Military control over the Middle East thus became a cornerstone in the defence policies of the West. To facilitate this control, the European powers also needed to develop their political influence in order to suppress the 'internal subversion' that Moscow could instigate through the development of local communist parties. Indeed, in Greece, Iranian Azerbaijan, and Kurdistan, the Soviets almost succeeded, in the aftermath of World War II, in having the local communist parties, linked to the mother party in the USSR through the Comintern, take power in their respective countries.

Contrary to a widespread preconception, the Marxist doctrine became widely popular in the Middle East. Communist parties developed considerably in the region.

They were not only founded or directed by youths from ethnic and religious minorities (Kurds, Jews, and Christians), they also represented a perfect meeting place for the youth of bourgeois and aristocratic families, middle classes, trade union members, Christians, Jews, and Muslims, talented artists as well as prominent intellectuals. And as the Western countries accumulated faux-pas, such as their unconditional support for the creation of Israel and then their entry into close alliance with this new state, they worriedly saw the communist, but also the nationalist and anti-imperialist, parties gain intellectual influence and grow increasingly attracted to various forms of socialist regimes (Yugoslav, Russian, and Chinese).

On the other hand, the development of the oil industry in the Middle East turned the region into the world's largest reservoir of low-cost energy. Controlling it was thus vital to keep Western economies running. The Europeans dominated the exploitation of the Iraqi and Iranian oilfields, while the Americans acquired in 1945 the exclusive monopoly over the exploitation of the enormous Saudi reserves. In the early 1960s, the discovery of oil reserves multiplied in the Middle East, in particular in the small merchant and Bedouin principalities of the Arabian peninsula (Abu Dhabi, Qatar, and Kuwait). To facilitate the transfer of oil to Europe and the Americas, pipelines were built to convey the precious liquid from the waters of the Persian Gulf and northern Mesopotamia in Iraq (Kirkuk) to the Mediterranean, through the Syrian, Lebanese, and Palestinian territories. Thus, the whole of the East became an area of vital interest to Western Europe and to the United States, but also to the Soviet Union, still haunted by its fears of being cornered by capitalists despite its many victories and conquests. Controlling the Middle East, hitherto an exclusive Western domain, was indeed a paramount objective in Soviet foreign policy.

Initially, the USSR had massively supported the creation of a Jewish state in Palestine, as Stalin had indeed wrongly seen in Zionism, which was predominantly socialist and originated in Soviet-controlled Central Europe, a great revolutionary promise in a region of traditionally Anglo–French influence. But the Soviet Union lost interest in the new Israeli state in the mid-1950s and shifted its support to the Arab nationalist movements in their struggle to shake Anglo–French domination. Israel, meanwhile, soon found a natural and increasingly close ally in old colonial Europe. In 1956, the joint Suez expedition of the Israeli, British, and French armies attacked Egypt and occupied the Sinai as well as the entire area of the Suez Canal. This symbolized the definitive alignment of Israel with the 'Western camp', led, as of then, by the United States. The Soviet Union made a sensational entrance into the Middle Eastern scene by supporting Egypt and by threatening the Israeli–European coalition with military intervention. In order to limit the damage, the United States persuaded the Israeli and Anglo–French troops to evacuate the area, and to act instead as arbitrators in Middle Eastern affairs. The political and military positions of Europe were completely shattered, making way for the United States and the USSR, the two new superpowers that now stood head to head in the Middle East.

This is the reason why the Arab–Israeli conflict subsequently attained increasingly acute proportions and political instability ultimately pervaded the whole region. The contradictory actions of the two superpowers were to hinder any form of regional cooperation, despite the pressing need for it to bring stability and economic growth to the region. In parallel, the Arab–Israeli conflict was to reach tragic dimensions in Lebanon, dragging the country into a maelstrom of violence (1975–1990), and the exploitation of Islam as a means to curb the expansion of communism in local societies was to constitute an additional and increasingly burdensome factor of instability on the states of the region. Last but not least, the dramatic fluctuations of oil prices between 1973 and 1985 were also to produce their share of adverse effects and to bring severe socio-economic and political repercussions.

The uncontrollable Arab–Israeli conflict and the Nasserite epic

Coups in Egypt and Syria, and Western attempts to build a military alliance

As was covered earlier, the defeat of the Arab armies to the Jewish militias in Palestine in 1948 brought about the collapse of the governments in Syria (1949) and Egypt (1952). In these two countries, where democratic life was intense, honed in the struggle against French and British colonial domination, the military took over with the support of the Western powers. The purpose was to contain and control the nationalist parties, the communist parties, and the Muslim Brotherhood, a religious anti-Western and anti-democratic conservative movement founded in 1928 in Egypt and backed by Saudi Arabia. The United States believed then that by building strong military regimes, it would be able to form an anti-Soviet coalition comprising the major states of the Middle East, including Israel. But Egypt, under the charismatic direction of Gamal Abdel Nasser, was to veto any military pacts with the West, conditioning its acceptance of such pacts on the definitive settlement of the conflict with Israel and on the full withdrawal of British troops from Egypt. Even though the idea of accepting the creation of Israel was already gaining ground in the Arab countries, its full acceptance was nevertheless conditioned on the return of the tens of thousands of Palestinian refugees to their ancestral territory. Egypt and Syria strived to develop their military expertise to avoid another crushing defeat to Israel, and also sought substantial foreign aid to develop their economies.

The United States, on the other hand, conditioned its military and economic aid on the normalization of Arab–Israeli relations and the entry of the Arab countries in a military alliance with Iran and Pakistan against the Soviet Union. While Iraq, Jordan, and Lebanon seemed ready to accept unconditional pro-Western alignment, Egypt and Syria resisted and, from 1955, developed increasingly close ties with the USSR in return for armament and economic aid. The Cold War slowly took root and polarized the Arab countries, and the League of Arab States – created in 1944 to serve as an institution of inter-Arab dialogue – became subdued by increasingly acute tensions.

The Suez expedition in 1956 stirred up a hornet's nest in the region. Nasser emerged from the Suez crisis with increased prestige throughout the Arab world and in 1958, Syria united with Egypt in a great moment of Arab nationalist fervour. The same year, Iraq underwent a military revolution that toppled the country's pro-Western monarchy; Jordan vacillated; and Lebanon witnessed a small-scale civil war that led the United States to disembark its troops on the beaches of Beirut. From 1958 to 1967, Nasser was to remain the foremost figure of the Middle East, skilfully playing Washington against Moscow, and contributing to the creation of a Nonalignment Movement, which comprised countries of the Third World seeking some influence on the international scene. Despite the collapse of the Syro-Egyptian union due to a Syrian counter-revolution in 1961, Nasserist Egypt, acclaimed and supported by Moscow, still dominated and influenced the entire Middle East. In 1962, it inspired a military revolution in Yemen, until then under the rule of an obscurantist monarchy, and rushed an Egyptian military contingent to rally round the rebellious young officers in their struggle; soon after, revolutionary movements flourished across the Arabian peninsula and threatened the Anglo–American military domination and control of oil.

The War of June 1967

It was the Arab–Israeli war of 1967 that brought Nasserite power to an end and allowed the United States to secure a progressive clamping down of Soviet influence in the Middle East. This retreat was accelerated by the war of October 1973 and the rise to power of Saudi Arabia and Iran (still under the domination of Shah Mohammed Reza Pahlavi), the loyal allies of the United States in the Middle East.

Intoxicated by its own power, Egypt found itself caught, in the spring of 1967, in a dangerous Arab–Israeli game of one-upmanship, led by Syria and Israel, whose borders were experiencing increasingly violent military skirmishes. By barring Israeli ships from using the Gulf of Aqaba in May 1967, Egypt gave Israel, which was supported by the United States, a pretext to wage another full-scale military offensive. Within only three days, the Israeli army captured the Sinai and the entire zone of the Suez Canal, in addition to the Syrian Golan Heights. The Arab defeat bore out the failure of the Soviet weapons used by the Syrian and Egyptian armies. As for the Jordanians, who also had the misfortune of taking part in the battle, they lost all of the West Bank as well as the Arab part of Jerusalem in just twenty-four hours.

In the aftermath of the 'Six-Day war', the victory of Israel was overwhelming and the infamous failure of the Egyptian and Syrian regimes, close to Moscow, absolute. Soviet efforts to rearm Egypt came to nothing: the war of attrition waged by the Egyptian army for two years on the Suez Canal led to heavy human losses, but failed to shake the uncontested superiority of the Israeli army. The latter was over-equipped by the United States after France, under General Charles de Gaulle, came round to the Arab position and imposed an embargo on weapons shipments to Israel. Nasser died, exhausted, in September 1970, after ending this war of attrition and agreeing to negotiate with the United States. This earned him severe criticism from the armed movements of Palestinian resistance, which he himself had backed in the past and which were now heading the very bureaucratic Palestine Liberation Organization (PLO), founded in 1964 under the sponsorship of the Arab League. Thereafter, Soviet influence was only exerted through some of these resistance movements, mainly the Popular Front for the Liberation of Palestine, headed by Dr George Habash, and its dissident wing known as the Democratic Front for the Liberation of Palestine, led by Nayif Hawatmeh.

The emergence of armed Palestinian movements

The armed Palestinian movements, more or less supported by Fatah, the organization of Yasir Arafat, the leader of the PLO from 1968, attempted a coup in Jordan in September 1969; the Popular Front meanwhile carried out notorious hijackings of Western airliners in Jordan, and later of an El-

Al airliner in Uganda, not to mention the Munich Olympic attacks in 1972. Brutally expelled from Jordan by the army (in what came to be known as 'Black September'), the Palestinian resistance movements took refuge in Lebanon, where they won the right to operate against Israel from bases in southern Lebanon. But the Palestinian operations from Lebanon prompted massive reprisals from the Israeli army against Lebanese and Palestinian civilians alike. The Israeli offensives plunged the small Lebanese republic, which had so far remained outside the conflict, into a period of increasing instability which, in turn, led to an alliance between the Lebanese 'progressive' parties (the Communist Party, the Organization of Lebanese Communists, the Progressive Socialist Party, the Syrian Socialist Nationalist Party) and the Palestinian movements of the PLO. This alliance was openly supported by Moscow (its leader, Kamal Jumblatt, the leader of the Socialist Party and the foremost Druze figure, was the winner of the 'Lenin Peace Prize' in 1972). Lebanon, one of the most loyal Western bastions in the Middle East, was on the verge of falling under the Soviet sway.

In Syria, General Hafiz al-Assad, Minister of Defence, was gradually emerging as a 'moderate'. In 1970, a coup enabled him to seize power and to eliminate the leftist wing of the ruling Ba'th Party. In Iraq, Saddam Hussein also rose to power and consolidated the Iraqi branch of that party by eliminating communists and Nasserists. He claimed to be the leader of Arab anti-imperialism and anti-Zionism, but clashed with another claimant for the mantle of Arab leadership, Syria. The rivalries between those two regimes, adhering to the same ideology of Arab unity, were to become a permanent feature of the Middle Eastern landscape and to complicate any coordination within the Arab League.

The war of October 1973, the rise of Saudi Arabia, and the implosion of Lebanon

In Egypt, President Anwar al-Sadat, who succeeded Gamal Abdel Nasser in 1970, eagerly pursued two main objectives: ending the Arab–Israeli conflict and drawing foreign investment into Egypt to pull the country from the economic stagnation and the state of exhaustion into which Nasser's policies had plunged it. As of 1972, he expelled numerous Soviet experts from Egypt, a clear signal to the United States of his willingness to join the Western camp. However, in October 1973, in coordination with the Syrian army and with support from Saudi Arabia, a close American ally, Sadat broke the military status quo on the Suez Canal in effect since 1969 when the Egyptians bravely succeeded in crossing the Canal. Caught unawares by this surprise attack, the Israeli army lost all its strategic positions; it also had to face a simultaneous attack from the Syrian army aimed at re-conquering the Golan Heights, lost in 1967. Moreover, the Arab oil-exporting countries, under the aegis of Saudi Arabia, imposed a selective and partial embargo on petroleum shipments to pro-Israeli countries. The price of oil, already strained since the early 1970s, skyrocketed from USD 3 to USD 11 per barrel. This enabled Saudi Arabia, the leading oil producer, to become a real financial power, counterbalancing its political weakness and enabling it to render acceptable its suffocating regime of Islamic fundamentalism.

The October War fuelled the Cold War in the Middle East. The United States, whose foreign policy had become much more aggressive and active under the Nixon–Kissinger tandem, conducted a gigantic airlift to enable the Israeli army to counterattack Egypt and Syria. The Soviets raised the tone by threatening to deploy their troops in Egypt, but it was already too late. President Sadat had accepted a ceasefire agreement and the start of military negotiations with Israel under American sponsorship. The Syrian army thus found itself alone in battle. In sum, the American objective of breaking Arab solidarity and of dealing with the different fronts of the Arab–Israeli conflict separately was successfully achieved.

Heavy pressure on Saudi Arabia led it to quickly lift its petroleum embargo, even before the end of hostilities on the Syrian Golan front. President Hafiz al-Assad was compelled to sign a ceasefire agreement in the spring of 1974, but American diplomacy did not care to go any further with Syria, which continued fostering close relations with the USSR. The United States mainly focused on improving relations with Egypt, because it found in President Sadat a docile interlocutor, ready to sign a separate peace agreement with Israel. In order to fight the Arab Nasserist, communist, and nationalist movements hostile to his policy, the Egyptian president encouraged a strong resurgence of the organizations of the Muslim Brotherhood in universities and trade unions. But his policy eventually brought his own downfall, as he was assassinated in October 1981 by a small Muslim extremist group, three years after the signing of the Camp David Agreements which sealed the Israeli-Egyptian peace and led to the Israeli withdrawal from Egypt and to the demilitarization of the Sinai, now under American control.

In fact, as of 1975, the Arab–Israeli conflict, frozen on the Syrian front and on the path towards resolution with Egypt, was shifted exclusively to Lebanese territory. Arab aid in support of the Palestinian resistance movements implanted in Lebanon poured into the country, allowing those movements to set up a virtual state-within-a-state and to extend their control over increasingly vast Lebanese territories. The magnitude and the brutality of the Israeli reprisals against Lebanon, and the passivity of the small Lebanese army, completely discredited the Lebanese state. The likelihood of Lebanon yielding to the Palestinian organizations, coalescing with the Lebanese 'progressive' parties under the Soviet umbrella, increased dramatically and sounded the alarm in the pro-Western Arab countries that had been supporting the Palestinian movements in Lebanon. Their answer to this new threat was to lend their military and financial support to the Phalanges as well. The Phalangist Party, a right-wing party with fascistic tendencies, decided to retaliate against the excesses of the Palestinian presence in Lebanon by using force. Although this was a minor party in the Lebanese Parliament, the Phalangist Party openly presented itself as the protector of the Christian communities against a coalition whose objective, according to the Phalanges, was to break Muslim–Christian coexistence in the country.

Hostilities broke out in Lebanon in the spring of 1975 and did not ease until 1990. Warfare was to become inherent to the Lebanese landscape, accentuated by the flaring of regional tensions. Indeed, Lebanon was taken hostage by the main protagonists on the Middle Eastern scene. The Syrian army was first to enter Lebanon, in early 1976, with Phalangist and American blessing but against Soviet wishes. The objective was to put an end to the subversive dynamics of the so-called 'Palestinian–progressive' forces, which was achieved with the capitulation of the Palestinian camp of Tall al-Za'tar in Beirut, a highly symbolic area for Palestinian left-wing organizations. However, the Palestinian dynamic still endured in southern Lebanon, leading Israel to invade the areas held by the Palestinian movements in 1978. The UN troops that were deployed in Lebanon then, acting under the instructions of the Security Council, failed to obtain the full retreat of the Israeli army. Rather, Israel waged another offensive in 1982, supported this time by the United States, with the firm intention of eradicating both the Syrian and the Palestinian presence from Lebanon, which it sought to turn into a satellite state. For three months, from June to August, the part of Beirut that was held by the Palestinian–progressive forces was savagely bombarded from air, land, and sea, thus depriving it of food, water, and power. The PLO was forced to evacuate Beirut and to transfer its headquarters to Tunis; a Phalangist government, buoyed by the United States and Israel, was brought to power in Beirut where American, French, and Italian military contingents were stationed to supervise the withdrawal of the Palestinian military. It is within this context that the Phalange Party, henceforth supported in the field by the Israeli army, perpetrated in September 1982 indiscriminate massacres of Palestinian and Lebanese civilians alike at the refugee camps of Sabra and Shatila, in reprisal for the assassination of Phalangist leader, Bashir Gemayel, who had been brought to the presidency by the Israeli–American coalition.

The Syrian riposte, this time supported by the USSR and Iran (where the Shiite clerics had seized power), was devastating: spectacular and deadly operations against Western contingents, massacres in the Shouf, forced displacements of those elements of the population supported by the Israeli army, then the main occupying power in Lebanon, and numerous abductions of Westerners. From 1983 to 1990, Lebanon was to know nothing but a state of anarchy that eventually left the country in utter exhaustion. The emergence of a government reconstituted through the Taif agreement, concluded in Saudi Arabia in October 1989, did nothing to reduce the encumbering Syrian, Israeli, and Iranian presence in Lebanon. The coalition of Lebanese leftist parties had disintegrated and given way to the birth of Druze and Shiite communitarian militias; by then, on the Christian front, the Phalanges and the militia known as the Lebanese Forces had become totally discredited, in particular after their violent confrontation with General Michel Aoun, the head of the Lebanese Army, who tried – unsuccessfully – between 1988 and 1990 to restore the country's sovereignty under his command.

The inexorable rise of radical Islam in the Middle East, the Iranian Revolution, and the Iran–Iraq war

Lebanon's fall into sectarianism only reflected the general rise of religious fundamentalism in the Middle East after the Arab defeat to Israel in 1967. In order to fight the expansion of communism in the region more effectively, the United States encouraged Saudi Arabia to mobilize Islam to contain Soviet influence. These efforts came to fruition in 1969 with the establishment of the Organization of the Islamic Conference (OIC) in Mecca. Owing to Saudi Arabia's financial power acquired since 1973, the OIC became a redoubtable rival to the virulently anti-American Nonalignment Movement, and to the Arab League, another anti-imperialist tribune. Saudi Arabia, alongside the Pakistani Islamic military dictatorship, was to shape the pillars of this organization. The stated goals of the OIC were to fight Marxist atheism, assert Islamic values, and promote solidarity among Muslim states. The Conference created several organisms designed to enforce solidarity (in economy, finance, and culture). Virtually everywhere, fundamentalist movements received substantial aid; and the appeal of generous Saudi subsidies, in addition to those of Kuwait and Qatar, led some countries to liquidate their socialist systems and to replace them with Islamic regimes devoted to cracking down on atheist communism.

The spectacular success of this policy drove the United States to support the rise to power of clerics in Tehran when the regime of the Shah was shaken in 1979. There was a great deal of fear that the coalition of leftist parties, in particular the powerful communist party (Tūdeh Party) and the Mojahedin-e Khalq, would take over Iran. Removed from his obscure exile in Iraq and settled in Paris, Imam Khomeini exploited the solicitude of the international media to affirm himself as the charismatic leader of the Iranian opposition. When the Shah of Iran in poor health abdicated the throne, the Imam was brought back from Paris to Tehran on the February 1, 1979, on a plane specially chartered by the French government, treating him like a real head of state. As soon as the Imam was settled, he embarked upon an anti-imperialist mobilization to reduce leftist opposition along with the old regime, which led to the notorious abductions of American diplomats in Tehran. The new regime engaged in a dangerous game of religious one-upmanship on both the regional and the international scene – a situation that neither superpower seemed to have predicted.

In December 1979, the USSR responded by invading Afghanistan to rally round the enfeebled yet favourable socialist regime. The United States was left with no other choice but to keep on reinforcing fundamentalist Sunnite and Shiite movements in all Muslim countries through its loyal allies, Saudi Arabia and Pakistan. The race to control the Middle East was open; Soviet positions grew untenable while Syria consolidated its alliance with Khomeinist Iran, which allowed it to shield itself from the destabilization being stoked by Sunnite Islamists within its borders. In 1980, Iraq, encouraged by Western governments and eager to assert its dominance over the Middle East, waged a devastating war against Iran in response to its numerous political and military provocations.

It was under Saddam Hussein, whose rule began in 1969 but only became absolute in 1974, that Iraq became an influential regional power enjoying the solicitude of the West. The Iraqi dictator presented himself as a modernist and a secular nationalist as the region lapsed into various forms of Islamism. In the 1970s, Iraq developed considerably, particularly in terms of education, health, and infrastructure. It even managed to conclude an agreement with France in 1979, giving it the right to build a nuclear plant for civilian purposes which Israeli warplanes bombed and destroyed in 1981. The Iraqi army was equipped with the most sophisticated weaponry provided by the European powers and the USSR; and finally, Iraq significantly developed its reserves and production of oil. In brief, this hitherto-marginal country became a key element in the region's future.

Nevertheless, Saddam Hussein's invasion of Iran proved to be a tactical miscalculation. It mainly profited the oil monarchies of the Gulf, now on the defensive due to Iran's subversive propaganda, but also the apprehensive American and European powers, which pushed him into warfare to counter the perceived threat of the Khomeinist regime. Indeed, Saddam Hussein seemed unaware that this time, he was attacking a much larger and more powerful country than his. After the thrill of the first Iraqi victories in Iran, the Iranian army counterattacked and advanced into Iraqi soil. The Western powers, mainly France and the United States, then provided Iraq with a whole array of weaponry including prohibited chemical weapons to countenance the Iranian incursion, but the war dragged on in a stalemate. It was not until July 1988 that Iran finally accepted a ceasefire. On both sides, the death toll (definitely over a million casualties) and destruction were immense.

7

THE FIRST GULF WAR AND ITS AFTERMATH

Iraq under trusteeship

Iraq emerged from the war with Iran overly indebted and overly armed at the same time. This increased Saddam's ire against another neighbour: the much more modest but very wealthy state of Kuwait – which was also coveted by Iran. Open warfare began in response to Kuwait's refusal to cancel the Iraqi debt, to rectify its borders to reinforce Iraq's military positions vis-à-vis Iran and to halt excessive pumping from Al-Rumaylah oil field, lying on the Iraqi–Kuwaiti borders. On August 2, 1990, the Iraqi army invaded Kuwait, but the Western response to this attack was a disproportionate U.S.-led military riposte against Iraq, marking the sudden abandonment of a dictatorial and tyrannical regime that had been supported without scruples for nearly twenty years. The military intervention carried out by the United States and its allies (France, the United Kingdom, Canada, the Netherlands, and a large number of Middle Eastern states such as Saudi Arabia, Turkey, Egypt, and Syria) was legitimized by a set of UN resolutions authorizing the use of force. This led to the landing of a contingent of 500,000 men in Saudi Arabia, to a massive bombing of all Iraqi infrastructures, and to a lightning campaign in January–February 1991, which resulted in the expulsion of Iraqi troops from Kuwait and in heavy casualties among the Iraqi contingents retreating in dismay.

The Western powers simultaneously encouraged the Kurdish revolt carried out in northern Iraq without granting it military support. This resulted in the killing of untold numbers of Kurds and in increased repression and turmoil in Turkish Kurdistan; they also encouraged Shiite rebellions in the south of the country, which were repressed with a heavy hand. But while the Western states created a restricted zone in northern Iraq, into which Iraqi troops were not authorized to penetrate, thus allowing the emergence of an embryonic Kurdish state, the Shiite rebels were not as fortunate: fearing the possible emergence of a Shiite state under Iranian control within Iraq, the Arab members of the alliance urged the U.S. armed forces not to intervene and the Shiites were abandoned to their fate. Saddam Hussein's troops were permitted to enter this region, where they ruthlessly suppressed the rebellion in the population of southern Iraq.

The Iraqi regime was able to survive its defeat. The Middle East, however, became even more fragile after this new direct Western intervention – facilitated by the definitive fall of the Soviets in the region, to the greatest regret of Saddam Hussein, who had been counting, wrongly, on his Soviet patron to prevent the deployment of allied forces of the Western military coalition to liberate Kuwait. But it was the neighbouring Arab countries and Turkey that intervened to dissuade the American president from letting the coalition troops advance into Baghdad to change the regime, or even to dismember the country along the lines of the two rebellions: Kurdish to the north and Shiite to the south. There were fears in Egypt and in the countries of the Arabian peninsula that the Iranian regime, which had proclaimed itself the protector of the Shia Muslims and was even sheltering a part of the opposition to the Iraqi regime, would gain more influence in the Arab states; whereas Turkey, overwhelmed by growing Kurdish nationalist claims, feared the creation of an autonomous Kurdish zone on its borders.

Another alarming factor during that period was the rise of Islamist movements everywhere without knowing who controlled them. Shortly after the first 'Gulf War', a series of terrorist attacks, one of which targeted an American military camp, struck at the very heart of the Saudi kingdom. The presence of U.S. troops on Saudi soil, just a few kilometres away from Islam's holy cities, aroused vehement anti-American sentiments among the Islamic fundamentalists, especially that the foreign troops did not withdraw from the Arabian peninsula even after successfully completing their mission. Saddam Hussein skilfully took advantage of this malaise to counter his Arab and Iranian opponents who had been criticizing his 'impious' regime. He showed increased religious fervour by leading his hitherto 'secular' regime down the path of Islamic piety and by inscribing Islamic faith assertions on the Iraqi flag. This new policy resulted in the deterioration of the condition of Iraqi women, although Iraq, alongside Tunisia, had been one of the leading Arab countries in the promotion of women's rights.

A far more ominous turnaround occurred at the end of the first Gulf War: terrorist groups pledging allegiance to Osama bin Laden, the Saudi hero of the Afghanistan liberation war, who had recruited, with support from the United States, Saudi Arabia, and Pakistan, thousands of young Arabs to fight the Soviet army, were growing increasingly active. Following the liberation of Afghanistan, they were sent off to fight in the Balkan countries (Bosnia and Kosovo), where Yugoslavia had crumbled into several states, but also in Russia (Chechnya). Until then, their actions had been in line with Western post-Cold War policies, but as of the mid-1990s, they directed their weapons against the United States and targeted American embassies in Kenya and Tanzania in 1998. Bin Laden thus became the world's most wanted man, in particular after the notorious and tragic 9/11 attacks on New York and Washington in 2001.

The impossible emergence of a Palestinian state

On the Palestinian front, the United States, encouraged by its successful lightning campaign to liberate Kuwait, sponsored formal talks between Israel and the Arab countries in Madrid. A heavy and complex peace process was set in motion, but to no avail. In 1993, the 'Oslo Agreement', signed with great pomp and circumstance at the White House by the PLO and Israel, deeply moved the entire world. The agreement granted the Palestinian leaders living outside their homeland the right to return to the West Bank and Gaza, but failed to achieve the Israeli evacuation of the Palestinian occupied territories. Furthermore, these agreements were extremely asymmetrical, imposing restrictions only on the newly created Palestinian Authority, while allowing Israel to keep on colonizing the West Bank and Gaza. This continued Israeli occupation led to the resurgence of a Palestinian armed resistance, giving Israel a pretext to further delay its full evacuation.

Endless negotiations were held regarding the extent of the withdrawal and the potential borders, but diplomacy fell short of reaching a consensus. The status of the Arab parts of Jerusalem and the Palestinian refugees' right of return – stipulated by a UN resolution and ratified by the General Assembly – were the two major stumbling blocks in this peace process. Another obstacle was the future of the Israeli settlements, which had developed significantly since the beginning of the Israeli occupation in 1967. The map of the West Bank came to look like a leopard skin with Jewish settlements scattered virtually everywhere, and the Israeli state had even built links to connect these different settlements both to each other and to Israel proper. It was therefore becoming increasingly difficult to envisage the creation of a Palestinian state without Israel dismantling its numerous settlements lying far beyond the original border between Israeli territory and the West Bank.

But over the years, the Israeli state has become accustomed to being an occupying state constantly waging reprisal operations. The situation worsened in 1995, with the assassination of Israeli Prime Minister Yitzhak Rabin, the co-signatory of the Oslo Agreement with Shimon Peres, by a young Israeli settler who opposed the cession of occupied Palestinian territories. This discouraged future Israeli governments from appearing to be more cooperative. For their part, Western countries have been increasingly uncritical of the Israeli policy; the United States, in particular, has systematically vetoed any condemnation of Israel at the United Nations Security Council. No Western power has intervened directly or even indirectly, via United Nations peace keeping forces, as was the case with South Africa, Rhodesia, Namibia, and later East Timor, as well as Bosnia and Kosovo (UN, Nato or European forces), to protect the occupied Palestinian population or to grant it back its right to self-determination and to an independent state.

The Palestinians' operations against Israelis and the ensuing massive Israeli reprisals brought about an interminable cycle of violence. But after the PLO's nationalist and secular movements had become subdued, the responsibility for Palestinian attacks was largely claimed by new, self-proclaimed Islamic militant organizations. As of 1996, those attacks took the form of suicide bombings inspired by the Sri Lankan Tamil guerrillas, sometimes striking at the heart of Israel's major urban centres. To Israel and most of the Western powers, such attacks were but a particularly perverse manifestation of terrorism that had to be combated relentlessly. The first anti-terrorist summit was held in the Egyptian city of Sharm el-Sheikh in 1996, bringing together the heads of state of the Arab world, the United States and Europe.

In September 2000, a provocative visit by General Ariel Sharon to the famous Al-Aqsa Mosque in Jerusalem (the third holiest place in Islam) was to re-ignite the Palestinian Intifada. The Israeli army re-invaded the areas of the West Bank and Gaza that it had evacuated, destroyed the infrastructure of the Palestinian Authority, the state-embryo that stemmed from the Oslo Agreement, and came down heavily on the Palestinian uprising.

The re-ignition of conflicts in the Middle East despite Soviet decline

The hopes engendered in the 1990s by the Madrid Conference and the Oslo Agreement evaporated. Yet, after the Gulf War and the liberation of Kuwait, President George H. W. Bush had promised a new international order to put a stop to violations of international law. In 1992, Shimon Peres had also raised high hopes with his vastly publicized book *The New Middle East*, in which he pictured the creation of a zone of free trade and prosperity in the Middle East, a vision encouraged by the American administration. But Peres also denounced Islamic terrorism, depicted in his book as a relic of irrational behaviour in Muslim societies that is totally extraneous to the ongoing occupation of the Palestinian territories conquered in 1967[19] – a hardly realistic theory.

---

[19] Shimon Peres with Arye Naor, *The New Middle East* (New York: Henry Holt & Company, 1993).

In Lebanon, the end of hostilities between the various Lebanese militias and rival factions in 1990 came at a costly price. The country was placed under Syrian trusteeship with American consent, as Syria's reward for joining the Western military coalition formed to oust the Iraqi army from Kuwait. General Michel Aoun, the commander in chief of the official Lebanese army, was forced into exile after launching an operation in 1989 to rid the country of the armed militias that had been spreading terror since 1975, an operation that was transformed into a war of liberation against Syria's military stranglehold. This initiative was mainly supported by France and Iraq, but it eventually failed due to the regional wind of change brought about by the invasion of Kuwait. General Aoun was left in the lurch after the United States gave the green light to a Syrian offensive that drove him out of the Presidential Palace where he had taken residence after being appointed prime minister by President Amin Gemayel, whose presidential mandate had expired in September 1988 (although the Lebanese parliament had failed to elect a successor at that time). Thus, Lebanon remained, for some time, in a state of political vacuum, with not one official president but two contending governments: a new cabinet formed by General Aoun and an outgoing cabinet refusing to cede power to its successor.

On the other hand, the wind of change brought about by the invasion of Kuwait proved somewhat favourable as it allowed the various Lebanese armed factions to reach a settlement in the adoption of a vast program of constitutional reforms, after Lebanese deputies met in Taif, Saudi Arabia, and adopted a Document of National Consensus. This agreement was signed in September 1989 under Saudi–American sponsorship, and endorsed by a United Nations Security Council declaration. It provided for the restructuring of the traditional distribution of constitutional powers and duties between president, prime minister, and speaker of parliament. Thus, shortly after parliament ratified the Taif agreement, a new president was elected in November 1989, but he was assassinated a few days later before even assuming office. Parliament gathered again and elected another president. General Aoun had meanwhile dissolved the National Assembly, in a last attempt to prevent irreversible Syrian control of Lebanon, but his decision was ignored. With the Syrian offensive thus underway, Aoun was forced to take refuge in the French embassy in Beirut in October 1990, and a few months later he was transferred to France where he remained in exile for fifteen years.

The new Lebanese political regime then quickly came under the control of a single man, Rafic Hariri, a Saudi-Lebanese billionaire, who fostered close ties with Syria, the Saudi king, as well as with the future French president, Jacques Chirac (who was to offer him blind friendship and unconditional support). Hariri was appointed prime minister in 1992 and he remained in office until 2004, with an interruption of twenty-two months between December 1998 and October 2000. During his term, he became the object of an extensive cult of personality which portrayed him as a philanthropist builder and an exceptional political leader. Ironically, however, it was also during his term that corruption festered and reached unparalleled proportions in Lebanon. His successive cabinets built up a colossal debt borrowed for reconstruction works (amounting to a staggering USD 35 billion by the end of 2004), out of which only about USD 6 billion were in effect absorbed by the reconstruction plan during this period, and while a public debt of merely USD 2 billion was inherited from the 15-year civil war (1975–1990).

Israel continued to occupy South Lebanon until May 2000, when Ehud Barak's government deemed it could no longer afford this costly occupation in light of the heavy losses inflicted on the occupying Israeli army by Hezbollah resistance fighters. Meanwhile, however, Israel massively raided other parts of South Lebanon for several days, first in 1993 and again in 1996. These two major offensives resulted in the displacement of tens of thousands of families and in the killing of untold numbers of Lebanese civilians in the targeted areas. Hezbollah emerged with increased prestige owing to its success at expelling the Israeli troops from South Lebanon, and became thereby a key architect in domestic politics. As of 1992, Hezbollah had also managed to secure several parliamentary seats in successive Lebanese elections, and even joined the government with two ministers for the first time in 2005.

As can be seen, the fall of the USSR in 1989–1990 did not bring stability back to the Middle East. The Arab regimes that were allied or close to the USSR (Syria, Libya and Iraq) were able to survive its demise. And, contrary to what the United States and numerous Western analysts had predicted, the end of the Soviet giant did not put an end to the Middle East's teething troubles, as those essentially sprang from the dismembering of the Ottoman Empire, from Western oil ambitions, and from Israel's occupation of Arab territories not only in the West Bank and Gaza, but also in Syria (the Golan Heights) and Lebanon (large parts of South Lebanon until 2000, in addition to the border-region of 'Shebaa Farms'). The Iranian regime, a product of the 'religious' revolution led by Imam Khomeini, toned down with the successive elections of the pragmatic Hashemi Rafsanjani, who headed the Iranian Republic after Khomeini's death in 1989 until 1997, and later of the exceptionally cultured

Muhammad Khatami from 1997 to 2005. Nevertheless, the United States, still deeply affected by the humiliating memory of the 1979 Iran hostage crisis where U.S. diplomats were held hostage in Tehran, continued to eye Iran with suspicion and sustained the sanctions imposed upon the country, still regarded as a sponsor of terrorism.

Up until that time, it had been good form to presume that Soviet hands were behind those Arab governments labelled as 'radical' that supported terrorism and refused to acknowledge the existence of the state of Israel. After the Iranian revolution, the subversive Khomeinist threat was added, in the eyes of the Western leaders, to that of the Soviets. However, the 9/11 attacks against New York and Washington in 2001, attributed to the al-Qaeda terrorist network, were to bring about new sweeping transformations in a Middle East still as unstable at the end of the 1990s as it had been after the fall of the USSR.

8

THE NEW MIDDLE EAST UNDER AMERICAN CONTROL: HEGEMONY, DEMOCRACY, AND TERRORISM

Forced democratization?

In reality, it was the personality of the new American president elected in 2000, George W. Bush, son of former U.S. president George H. W. Bush who had coordinated the military campaign to liberate Kuwait, just as much as the notorious 9/11 attacks, that made tensions and violence flare again in the Middle East. The neoconservative hawks forming the new U.S. administration aspired to remodel the Middle East, which seemed to be the only region still resisting the wave of democratization that, more or less towards the end of the Cold War, came upon Asia, Latin America, and Africa. The European Union also sought to achieve this goal through the Euro-Mediterranean Partnership (or Barcelona Process), launched in 1995 to create a Euro-Mediterranean free-trade zone by reinforcing the rule of law and by establishing a competitive free market economy. What was more disturbing, however, was the popularity among American neoconservatives of scholar Samuel Huntington's thesis about a clash of world civilizations, likely to lead the Western world and Islamic civilization, and later Asian Confucianism, into opposition. First published in 1992 in American magazine *Foreign Affairs*, Huntington's thesis was developed and republished the following year in a work that acquired worldwide notoriety.

Upon his accession to power, President Bush declared that the United States would no longer focus on the Arab-Israeli conflict, because, according to his team, the region's real problems were terrorism, Iran, and the weapons of mass destruction allegedly owned by Iraq in spite of the draconian UN regime of embargo and international inspections imposed on the country. The 9/11 attacks provided clear evidence of that vision of the world in the eyes of the new American administration. It thus paved the way for U.S. pre-emptive wars and for the invasion of Afghanistan, lying at the extreme end of the Middle East, accused of harbouring the notorious bin Laden and his terrorist organization, and later of Mesopotamia, located at the very heart of the Arab world. In fact, the invasion of Iraq in March 2003 seemed to complete what the first Gulf War had failed to achieve in 1991. To justify this invasion, President Bush claimed that Iraq possessed weapons of mass destruction, although no evidence of such weapons was ever found as was later demonstrated by an official American report that was issued nine months after the invasion. Another reason for the invasion stated by President Bush was the will to rebuild the Middle East on democratic and stable grounds.

On November 6, 2003, six months after the invasion and occupation of Iraq, he publicly announced the launching of an initiative to promote freedom and democracy in the Middle East, pompously labelled the 'Greater Middle East'. In June 2004, this initiative became known as the 'Broader Middle East and North Africa Initiative' (BMENA). The aim was to create a 'Forum for the Future' that would bring together the leaders of the states of the Middle East, industrialised countries of the Group of Eight (G8), and the region's businesses and civil society groups, to discuss reforms. The BMENA initiative was launched at the G8 Sea Island Summit hosted by the United States in June 2004, in the presence of a few Middle Eastern heads of state who were invited to attend this summit. The agenda included providing assistance to promote democratic institutions in the region, promoting access to capital for micro-enterprises, sponsoring teacher-training specialized in fighting illiteracy, providing business-training for female entrepreneurs, and injecting USD 100 million to finance small and medium-sized enterprises. The leading Western countries all seemed to have their hearts set on launching reform initiatives in the Arab world. Egypt and Yemen held solemn conferences for the promotion of democracy and 'governance' – the latest term in vogue – in Arab countries; and even the Arab League sang the same tune of reform and governance, declaiming this leitmotif at a head of state summit held in Tunis on May 22–23, 2004.

But at the same time, while the Arab regimes were previously accused of brutally repressing Islamic movements in contempt of the basic principles of human rights, they were now suddenly enjoined to totally eradicate such movements, even when the latter formed the backbone of their power, as is the case with Saudi Arabia, or participated in its parliamentary life, like Hezbollah in Lebanon. This was also the case when Hamas won the majority of seats in the Palestinian elections held in January 2006.

Under such conditions, it was not surprising that both the appeals for democracy and reform in the Arab world and the military and political pressures exerted by the United States, with the help of several European allies, have ultimately failed to produce the results expected by the West. The process was in fact reminiscent of the *Tanzimat* era in the 19th century, when the European colonial powers had been calling for democratic reforms in the institutions of the Ottoman Empire such as proclaiming equality between Muslims and non-Muslims and protecting ethnic and religious minorities, while at the same time invading and occupying the Balkan and Arab provinces of the Empire. History shows that such hybrid and contradictory European interventions, both democratic and colonialist, only led to massacres and forced population displacements and exchanges during the First World War and its aftermath.

The Iraqi crisis: pre-emptive war and occupation

Numerous serious and certified testimonies, from both American and foreign sources, stated that the Bush administration actually intended to invade Iraq immediately after 9/11 – perhaps even earlier –, and that the alleged presence of weapons of mass destruction threatening world peace was nothing but a pretext. The real motives for the American invasion remain obscure and subject to diverse versions and speculations: the defence of Israel, the control of oil, the need to assert imperial power after the fading of Soviet influence, or perhaps a combination of all three. But whatever the motive for the invasion might have been, the aftermath on the ground was beyond the shadow of a doubt: new traumatic wounds in the already tormented and exhausted psyche of the peoples of the region, and a new spiral of violence and torment.

Reports regarding the state of absolute disrepair of Iraqi infrastructure and the general impoverishment of the population caused by the American invasion were extremely rare. The incursion completed the work of destruction of Iraqi society that had begun thirteen years earlier with the UN economic embargo, not to mention the countless forced displacements and massacres perpetrated by Saddam Hussein's authoritarian regime in the context of the permanent strife into which he had sunk the whole country since the start of hostilities with Iran in 1980. The way the United States invaded Iraq, turning a blind eye to the pillage of the country's institutions as well as its archaeological and cultural patrimony, and then dismantling the Iraqi army, police, and security services, can only be attributed to a barely conceivable degree of criminal recklessness from a power renowned for its military and civil strategy and management skills, or, most probably, to its desire to prevent Iraq from ever becoming truly independent again.

Even more troublesome was that the American colonizer followed in the very footsteps of the old European colonizer, playing the sectarian, ethnic, and regional cards to impose its dominance and arbitration. As had been previously the case in other countries – in Lebanon (the Maronite 'privileges') and Yugoslavia (Pan-Serb nationalism and the despotic Milosevic) –, the international media, once again, designated a scapegoat to be blamed for all Iraqi misfortunes. This time, it was the Sunnite religious community as well as Saddam Hussein and his clan who belonged to this community. The Shiites and the Kurds were portrayed as the only victims of dictatorship; sectarianism and ethnicism intensified, as the tribal chiefs and Shiite clergies became the sole local spokespersons in the eyes of the American invaders, to the detriment of the middle class nationalists and even the returning expatriates who had once formed the Iraqi opposition. The Iraqis, who had so far resisted sectarianism, were thus gradually embroiled in a latent Sunni–Shiite civil war that was attaining alarming proportions, while the rivalries between the Kurds, demographically ousted by Saddam's forced displacement policies, the Turkmen, and the Arabs were growing increasingly deadly in the northern cities.

In January 2005, the Iraqi elections served to crystallize this Sunni–Shia cleavage. While the Sunnites largely boycotted the ballot, the Shiites voted en masse and won the majority of seats. The Iraqis courageously voted, braving the threats of armed resistance movements, to pacifically affirm their existence in the face of the occupation. The founding of new institutions, including a new constitution laying the foundations for federalism, did nothing to halt or stop the cycle of violence. Oil plants were repeatedly sabotaged, police stations savagely attacked, places of worship and public squares targeted by car-bomb attacks, and the invading U.S. troops repeatedly assaulted. In response, the American army waged massive and collective reprisals against entire cities (such as Fallujah in 2004). Simultaneously, corruption festered among the American occupation authorities and their newly appointed Iraqi leaders, abductions and assassinations targeting foreigners and Iraqis alike multiplied, and the scandalous torture practised by U.S. soldiers in Iraqi prisons was revealed to the world: all of this turned the region into a notorious hotbed of tensions.

From the very first years of occupation, the American government had held the Iranian and Syrian regimes responsible for the bloody chaos that became ingrained in Iraq, and justified its continued presence in the region by pointing to the upsurge of terrorism, sometimes blamed on the former Ba'thist regime, sometimes on al-Qaeda, and sometimes on Iran and Syria, accused of sabotaging Iraq's stability. But the destabilizing effects of the process of American domination over the Middle East, designed and implemented by the Bush administration, were to spread well beyond the Iraqi borders.

Resolution 1559: destabilizing Lebanon and encircling Syria

In the spring of 2000, and after twenty-two years of Israeli occupation, the liberation of South Lebanon by Hezbollah finally allowed the country to enjoy some stability again, albeit still in the shadow of Syria's hegemonic presence, largely supported by the main local politicians. Paradoxically, the regional effects of the tragic 9/11 attacks ended up bringing normality to the country: the wealthy Arab tourists of the Arabian peninsula turned their backs on trendy European and American destinations, and came en masse to Lebanon, just as Hezbollah ceased its military operations. Capital also began pouring into the Lebanese banks, thus avoiding the thorough system of international inspections set up to trace terrorist funding, which often stemmed from the Arabian peninsula. At the same time, the Syrian military contingent stationed in Lebanon decreased from 40,000 to 14,000 soldiers between 2000 and 2004. As of 2001, Beirut regained its status as the capital of the Arab world, with the 2002 Arab League Summit and the Francophone Summit that was held in the Lebanese capital in 2003.

However, at the end of the summer of 2004, Lebanon was convulsed again. Tensions flared when key Lebanese prime minister, billionaire Rafic Hariri – who fostered particularly close relations with the Western states and the Syrian nomenklatura –, after having strongly opposed the extension of President Emile Lahoud's term, suddenly changed his position and pushed the Lebanese cabinet to ratify the constitutional amendment allowing the prolongation. Meanwhile, however, on the eve of that parliamentary session, the United Nations Security Council had adopted

Resolution 1559 under French sponsorship (September 2, 2004). This resolution stipulated that Lebanon should prevent the extension of the presidential term, that Syria should withdraw its troops from Lebanon, and that the government should disband and disarm all Lebanese and Palestinian militias still active in the country and deploy its army in South Lebanon. For the United States, the objective was two-fold: this resolution allowed putting an end to the Syrian protectorate over Lebanon – designed by the Americans themselves in 1990 – and the disarming of Hezbollah, although this organization was regarded by large segments of the Lebanese population as part of the Lebanese resistance despite its close ties with Iran and Syria. As a result, Lebanon was thrown back into the same situation as in 1975, when the hostility between the Palestinian resistance movements and their Lebanese allies, known as the 'progressive' parties on the one hand, and the conservative right-wing parties led by Christian political figures on the other, broke out in earnest.

Rafic Hariri, incontestably the most influential man on the political scene of the Middle East, was the first victim of this violent storm that blew over Lebanon. He was assassinated on February 14, 2005. His killing aroused unprecedented levels of indignation worldwide: never had the assassination of a prime minister triggered such intense international outcry, not even that of Aldo Moro in Italy or Olof Palme in Sweden. This tragic attack sparked vehement resentment in Beirut, where hundreds of thousands of young Lebanese flooded the streets in a series of spontaneous mass protests. They took over the historic Martyrs Square, where the corpse of the assassinated prime minister – celebrated more like a saint or a marabout – was buried, and demonstrated in perfect harmony. The 'Beirut Spring', reminiscent of the 'Orange Revolution' which had taken place shortly before in Ukraine, was launched to serve as an example for the other Arab peoples and to incite them to rise against tyranny. The last Syrian contingents left Lebanon in April in a general hue and cry. In an unprecedented outburst of activism, the United Nations Security Council established an International Investigation Commission to elucidate Rafic Hariri's assassination; it also created a Special International Tribunal for Lebanon and appointed a permanent UN representative in charge of implementing Resolution 1559 and reporting regularly on the progress of the investigation. In the meantime, Lebanon was undergoing a period of great instability: in the weeks that followed Hariri's death, a series of car-bomb attacks rocked the Christian areas of the country, and several prominent political and media figures were assassinated.

A year later, Lebanon was beset by a new tragedy. In the summer of 2006 when Hezbollah abducted two Israeli soldiers, Israel launched a major military offensive against Hezbollah, savagely bombarding South Lebanon, the Beqaa, and the southern suburbs of Beirut, where Hezbollah had its headquarters. This 33-day war took an alarming human toll: 1,300 Lebanese civilians were killed, 3,600 others were injured (against 43 killed and 101 injured on the Israeli civilian side) and some 900,000 were displaced. During the shelling, the Israeli armed forces tried to reinvade the Lebanese territories that Israel had occupied from 1978 to 2000, but the Hezbollah fighters showed remarkably stubborn resistance as their lines were only breached partially yet at a very costly price (117 Israeli soldiers were killed). Furthermore, despite the massive bombing of all its positions, the Lebanese resistance still managed to launch around 100 to 200 rockets daily at Galilee villages and as far as the city of

Haifa, which forced the inhabitants of those regions to hide in bomb shelters or to flee the targeted areas. Until then, not even a regular Arab army had been able to inflict such a crushing defeat upon the almighty Israeli army, with the exception of the first stages of the Arab–Israeli war of October 1973 in which, against all odds, the Egyptian army had been able to cross the Suez Canal and to break through the Israeli defence lines, before eventually being by-passed and encircled by Israeli troops in a surprise counter-attack.

The United States clearly encouraged the Israeli government to embark on this bloody adventure in Lebanon. Indeed, during the very first Israeli bombings of Lebanon in July, the U.S. Secretary of State, Condoleezza Rice, publicly described the plight of Lebanon as part of the 'birth pains' of the new Middle East that the American superpower sought to create. It was only when it became clear that the Israeli forces would not be able to eliminate Hezbollah militarily, nor to reinvade some part of South Lebanon, that the UN Security Council finally voted a resolution (1701, issued on 13th August 2006), brokered by the United States, demanding 'full cessation of hostilities'. This resolution also called for the reinforcement of the UNIFIL contingents (stationed in southern Lebanon since 1978), thus increasing overall troop strength from barely 2,000 to 15,000, and for the deployment of the Lebanese army along the borders with Israel.

This new war sparked, for symmetrical reasons, an acute political crisis in both Lebanon and Israel. In Israel, the army was severely criticized for its shortcomings, which led, in turn, to the dismissal of several high-ranking officers and to the establishment of a state commission of inquiry devised to probe the way the war had been waged. In Lebanon, Hezbollah's abduction of two Israeli soldiers was strongly denounced by the parties known as the 'March 14 Alliance', aligned with U.S. foreign policy in the Middle East. This polarization led to acute tensions within the Lebanese government which included Hezbollah representatives as well as their allies from the Shiite Amal party. The crisis degenerated in November 2006 due to the disaccord regarding the status of the international Lebanese tribunal devised to try the assassins of Rafic Hariri: the four ministers representing the Shiite community and one of the ministers representing the Greek-Orthodox community tendered their resignation, thus unbalancing the constitutionally required representativeness of the religious communities in the cabinet, and rendering it illegitimate. However, Prime Minister Fouad Siniora, and the other ministers, benefiting from Western support, refused to resign, which further polarized the country and gave rise to a dangerous constitutional crisis. Lebanon, like in 1975, was again thrown into the regional and international bloody geopolitical game of control over the Middle East.

The eternal recurrence of the Palestinian tragedy

During that time, the situation had seriously deteriorated on the Palestinian front. As of 2003, Israel and the United States had found a perfect scapegoat in Yasir Arafat for the failure of the Oslo Agreement and for the resurgence of the Palestinian Intifada in 2000. As a consequence, any improvement in terms of Palestinian rights was no longer dependent on Israel's withdrawal from the Palestinian occupied territories, but rather on the reform of the Palestinian Authority and the dismissal of its exhausted leader – albeit praised to the skies just a few years earlier. Israel's repression of the new Palestinian uprising resulted in bloodshed as usual. The Israeli army reinvaded the West Bank and the 'Gaza Strip', and destroyed the greater part of the Palestinian infrastructure built over the previous years thanks to international aid, mainly from the European Union. In response to the suicide attacks perpetrated by the Palestinian resistance fighters in Israeli cities, the Israeli government decided to build a 'separation wall' between the Israeli settlements in the West Bank and the Palestinian cities and villages. That wall further shrank the territories still owned by Palestinians and even cut some villages in half; in brief, it created a collective concentration camp. And although the International Court of Justice of The Hague strongly condemned the creation of the Israeli West Bank barrier in June 2004, the construction of the wall continued.

Meanwhile, pressured by the European countries and the Arab governments, the United States hastily drafted in June 2003 a 'roadmap' supposed to settle the conflict: the Palestinians would finally acquire an independent state within five years, provided they ceased resistance operations against Israeli occupation, undertook comprehensive reforms of their institutional apparatus, fought corruption and pledged to respect human rights. That roadmap was a new version of the Oslo or the Camp David Agreements, only differing by providing an even lesser guarantee of Palestinian rights than the previous two. But above all, this version made no mention of a possible end to the ever-expanding process of colonization chipping away, day after day, at what was left of the Palestinian territories.

In May 2005, Israeli Prime Minister Ariel Sharon announced a unilateral withdrawal from Gaza, thus suddenly appearing a 'man of peace', as he was described by President George W. Bush, because now, he was also faced with the revolt of the Israeli settlers on that petty piece of land. He was transformed into a 'moderate' in the Western public eye, though all experts on the Palestinian tragedy were well aware that the real motive behind such a manoeuvre was to better concentrate Israeli efforts on the colonization of the West Bank ('Judea and Samaria' in Israeli vocabulary), thus ruling out the possibility of ever founding a Palestinian state bearing that name. As they had for the Oslo Agreement and the Roadmap, the international media declaimed the same hypocritical chorus about a 'historic event' heralding a possible end to this tragic conflict. The same had happened at the signature of the equally 'historic' Wadi Araba Agreement in October 1994 by Israel and Jordan, and the Sharm el-Sheik Accords in February 2005, between Ariel Sharon and the head of the Palestinian Authority, Mahmoud Abbas – who assumed this position upon Yasir Arafat's mysterious death in December 2004. Like an old and timeworn movie, the same images were broadcasted worldwide, with pretty much the same actors and the same speeches on terrorism, justice, and democracy...

On the ground, the Israeli evacuation of Gaza did not change in any way the fate of the Palestinians in the evacuated land or in the West Bank. At the end of December 2008, the Gaza Strip, already under a full economic siege, was heavily bombarded by the Israeli army. As with Hezbollah in Lebanon in summer 2006, the Israeli government wrongly believed it could crush the Hamas resistance movement by force. However, it was another butchery of the Palestinian civilian population, including numerous children, and did not succeed in eradicating either Hamas or its capacity to resist.

Confrontation with Iran

The policy endorsed by the Bush administration did not prove more successful on the Iranian front. George W. Bush reinforced the aggressive U.S. containment policy that had continued against Iran even after Khomeini's death in June 1989 and despite the gradual normalization of political life in the country under the successive presidencies of more flexible and pragmatic figures, such as Hashemi Rafsanjani (1989–1997) and in particular, Muhammad Khatami (1997–2005). The latter was to express positive reformist and liberal aspirations and even act as a pioneer in the promotion of 'dialogue among civilizations' in an attempt to defuse the ravages caused by Samuel Huntington's 'Clash of civilizations'. While the European countries maintained dialogue and openness, the American government maintained economic sanctions against Iran. Furthermore, in January 2002, in a State of the Union address, George W. Bush included Iran in his 'axis of evil'. Consequently, Iran turned mainly to China and Russia for military hardware, which further fuelled American resentment.

Under such conditions, it was not surprising to see the change of mood in Iran with the election of Mahmoud Ahmadinejad in August 2005. Ahmadinejad easily defeated his rival, Hashemi Rafsanjani, who was again running for the presidency. The new president, the former mayor of Tehran, was a hands-on man, a partisan of social justice, rather indifferent to the arguments of the 'moderates' still seeking to build closer ties with the United States. He was considered to have close relations with the most conservative religious authorities and the guide of the Islamic Revolution, Ayatollah Ali Khamenei, Khomeini's successor. Seeing that his two predecessors had failed in their reformist efforts, he adopted an ostentatious and provocative stance regarding the West. He presented himself as a vigorous supporter of the Palestinian cause and the armed movements of resistance against Israel, such as Hamas and Hezbollah. He condemned the West for its unconditional support of the Israeli occupation of Arab territories, questioned the veracity of the Shoah, and even held an international seminar in Teheran to 'discuss' that matter. Last but not least, he proudly declared that Iran had begun enriching uranium and that the country would soon be mastering the entire nuclear field for peaceful purposes.

This greatly annoyed the United States and the countries of the European Union. On December 23, 2006, the United Nations Council voted a resolution (1737) against Iran's uranium enrichment program, imposing sanctions upon those responsible for the Iranian nuclear program. Moreover, the United States stepped up allegations against Iran, accusing the regime of supporting resistance against its occupation of Iraq.

A grave crisis was thus incubating in the Middle East, but it was attenuated toward the end of 2006 by two major events: the defeat of the Republicans in the November elections and the revelation in December of the harsh conclusions of the report of the 'Study Group on Iraq', co-presided by James Baker, George H. W. Bush's former Secretary of State, which called for a withdrawal of American troops from Iraq and the resuming of contacts with Iran and Syria to prevent further degradation of the situation in the country.

Turkey and its relations with the European Union

In contrast, throughout this period, Turkey appeared as a safe haven and a strong and respected state in a region beset by constant troubles, wars, and violence. The heritage of

Mustapha Kemal no doubt allowed this exception. Of course, the intrusion of the Turkish army, the guardian of the Kemalist tradition, in the country's political life appears a relic from a distant past when compared with European democratic standards. Such interventions have occurred each time leading army commanders saw a possible threat to the Kemalist heritage, incarnated sometimes by new political figures, sometimes by what the military deemed as unfit management of the state. They did not, however, prevent Turkish political life from modernizing and changing its face as of the 1980s, especially with the rise to power of the president of the Motherland Party, Turgut Özal, both a nationalist and a liberal figure, particularly in terms of the economy. Özal became prime minister in 1983 and was reinstated in his functions until 1987, before becoming the president of the Turkish Republic in 1989. He passed away in 1993.

It was under his long rule that the Welfare Party (Refah), a party with a strong Islamic tincture, developed, marking a novelty in a country that had always swaggered about its strictly secular regime. The Welfare Party swept 158 out of 550 seats in the legislature during the parliamentary elections of December 1995, and became thereby the first Islamic party to win a general election in Turkey. Its leader, Necmettin Erbakan, became prime minister in January 1996. But fears that the Welfare Party was attempting to Islamicize the country led the military to force Erbakan to resign in February 1997. Erbakan left office and the Welfare Party, accused of 'imperilling state secularism', was banned and dissolved by the Constitutional Court in January 1998. It re-emerged, however, under Recep Tayyip Erdoğan, as the Justice and Development Party. Although his party won the parliamentary elections in 2002 with an absolute majority of

363 seats, Erdoğan was legally barred from serving in parliament or as prime minister because of his 1998 conviction for 'inciting religious hatred' (after reciting a poem that compared public Islamic symbols to means of political resistance). A constitutional amendment, however, effectively removed Erdoğan's disqualification and allowed him to run again. On March 9, 2003, he won a by-election and became prime minister in March 2003. The military did not intervene this time and the new prime minister presented himself as a 'moderate' figure without undue difficulty.

During his term, Turkey made several improvements in terms of human rights and economic liberalism in the hope of joining the European Union, something which Turkey had been attempting since 1989, but which was only made official with the opening of negotiations in December 2004. However, several EU member states voiced their opposition to Turkey's membership: the European Union was already encumbered with numerous Muslim immigrants, mainly the Maghribis and the Turks, and the main concern was as to whether the Union could effectively embrace a population of 70 million additional Muslims. Many European politicians posed that question, not hesitating to voice their rejection of a membership that could, according to them, contribute to changing Europe's 2000-year-old Christian face. The fear of Islamic terrorism also influenced European public opinion although the Turkish regime had declared itself resolutely secular and despite the fact that the country had been itself targeted by numerous violent attacks at the hands of Islamist groups and the Kurdistan Workers' Party, the PKK. Its leader, Abdullah Öcalan, was arrested and sentenced to death in December 1999, but the sentence has not yet been carried out. The Kurdish question has remained a major problem for Turkey, especially in the framework of its efforts to comply with the criteria for membership of the European Union. This led to the lifting of the prohibition of speaking Kurdish in 1991 – but it was not until 2006 that a Kurdish radio station and two television channels were finally authorized to broadcast in Turkey.

The power vacuum in the Middle East

The appalling picture which emerges at the dawn of the 21st century is that of a Middle East subdued by turbulence for multiple complex reasons. Such reasons include the colonial trauma suffered by the Arab provinces of the Ottoman Empire, carved up between France and Britain; then the Anglo-Saxon hegemonic policy carried out in Iran at the time of the monarchy, but also its resentment of Nasserist Egypt, another leading country in the region. Another reason for this was the failure of the Arab regimes, after having gained their independence in the wake of World War II, to turn the Arab League into a nucleus of organic solidarity in the face of external challenges – the first being that of the Palestinian tragedy, which was triggered by the creation of the state of Israel in 1948 and the successive conquests of the Arab territories. But the Arabs also failed to unite in the face of the challenge posed by the East–West rivalry during the Cold War, some aligning with American policy, others with the Soviets, as covered earlier.

Arab disunity was no less significant regarding the Islamic revolution in Iran; it even led to a bloody war between Iran and Iraq that raged for eight years (1980–1988), and then to the equally ravaging conflict between Kuwait and Iraq, which allowed the United States to deploy its troops in the Arabian peninsula in 1990–1991, and to invade Iraq without difficulty in 2003. The Arab regimes have also remained divided as to their relationship with the Iranian regime, which acquired much prestige among the peoples of the region, largely by simply filling the power vacuum in the Arab world. In early times, that vacuum had attracted France and Britain, and later the United States and the USSR. The impotence of the regular Arab armies has also allowed the Israeli state to become a major military power and to continue colonizing the occupied Syrian Golan Heights, in addition to the West Bank.

This power vacuum is unlikely to be filled any time soon. Indeed, most of the Arab regimes have remained under strong American influence, and this has fanned internal instability as well as nationalist – and increasingly religious tinted – opposition (those who opposed this hegemony were strongly pressured by Western countries and were thus bound to rely on another power, as was the case when Syria concluded several agreements of economic and military cooperation with Iran). This evidently created a perfect breeding ground for the Wahhabist or Salafist-inspired terrorist organizations, which have shown no reluctance in waging several deadly attacks against many Arab countries (Egypt, Saudi Arabia, Morocco, Algeria, and Jordan), and various Muslim countries (Indonesia, Turkey, and Pakistan). But by amalgamating such organizations with other legitimate movements of resistance to the American and Israeli occupation of Arab territories, the policies endorsed by the United States, some European decision-makers, and even the United Nations, have only further exacerbated instability in the region.

Nevertheless, the general landscape is not all sinister. Oil resources have provided great prosperity for the small emirates of the Arabian peninsula, united in 1973 under the banner of the United Arab Emirates Federation (UAE).

Against all odds, the integration of seven small entities, each under the rule of an autocratic tribal chief, has fared marvellously well from both a political and an economic standpoint. The political canniness, the wisdom, and the strong personality of Sheikh Zayid al-Nahyan, the leader of the Abu Dhabi Emirate, who died in 2003, no doubt contributed to the success of that federative union, whereas all other attempts at uniting two or three Arab countries undertaken between 1961 and 1973 had miserably failed in the past. Another significant factor was the success of the Gulf Cooperation Council (GCC) founded in 1980 and comprising the UAE, Saudi Arabia, Qatar, Bahrain, Kuwait, and Oman. The GCC council succeeded in formulating similar regulations in various fields such as security and defence policies, but also economic strategies, financial markets, and customs duties; a monetary union is also likely to be created after the concretisation of a customs union. Also worth mentioning is the successful reunification of Yemen, long divided into two separate states; the first, to the north, was under Saudi influence, the other, to the south, was called the Democratic Republic of Yemen and had socialist tendencies and close ties with the USSR. After a first failed attempt, this union finally durably materialized in 1995.

However, apart from the Yemeni case, those successes were exclusively reserved to a limited club of very wealthy countries with low demographic density, united under the American umbrella. Furthermore, from an economic angle, despite its oil wealth, the Middle East's economic growth rates have remained weak, lagging far behind those achieved in others parts of the world (as will be shown in the next chapter).

In reality, in the Middle East, only three states bear the features of a strong state: Israel, Turkey (a NATO member), and Iran. But even the very existence of these three states faces many a challenge. The Israeli state has embroiled itself in a colonial and chronic expansionist policy, fostering relations of rare violence with its neighbouring Palestinian and Lebanese populations. The Turkish state is still struggling with the Kurdish crisis, especially after turmoil in Iraq paved the way for the emergence of a Kurdish autonomous 'state' in northern Iraq, on the Turkish border. Turkey is also struggling with a public opinion deeply torn between partisans of resolute secularism and the more general mood of withdrawal into Islam affecting the entire region. Lastly, the Iranian regime remains relatively isolated on the international scene; the balance between conservatives and liberals that is maintaining a bare minimum of pluralism in the country is very fragile, and the trusteeship of the religious class over Iran enjoys far from unanimous support, even among the clergy where the *Velayat Faqih* regime is largely contested, just like in all the other Muslim countries containing Shiite communities.

In sum, the chaotic management of the region is assured by the triangle formed by Israel, Turkey, and the United States (linked together by numerous agreements of military cooperation). The GCC countries, lacking an autonomous and significant military power, seem to passively follow the American–Israeli axis. This way of running the Middle East is strongly opposed by Iran, and, to a lesser extent, by Syria and the terrorist Jihadist and Takfirist groups, hostile to the American–Israeli hegemony – the former calling for a Holy War to repel the Christian and Jewish invaders, and the latter readily excommunicating all Muslims who refuse their doctrines, considering it necessary to physically eliminate them. Again, by no means should such groups be conflated with the movements of resistance against the military occupation of Iraq and Palestine, nor with Hezbollah, which aims to liberate Lebanese prisoners detained in Israeli prisons and to guarantee respect for Lebanese sovereignty, mainly by seeking to end Israel's occupation of the Shebaa Farms area, and its violations of Lebanese waters and air space.

Consequently, the return of peace and stability to this tormented part of the world is unlikely for the foreseeable future. At the dawn of the new millennium, the Middle East still appears to be an ever-unattainable construction. Its societies are consumed by violence, particularly the powerful kingdom of Saudi Arabia, which has been the target of terrorist attacks at the hands of the very same Islamists it had been taking under its wing since its founding. The Israeli–American domination might attain greater proportions, and the most brutal forms of colonialism develop into a chronic phenomenon. But this will only generate more terrorist violence; a violence whose primary victims will be Muslim societies, but also European societies – as evidenced by the Madrid attacks in March 2004 and the London attacks in July 2005.

The Middle East no doubt remains to this day a stormy region, where the Western powers are still deeply involved economically, politically, and militarily, due to their own history that led to the emergence of the State of Israel, and to their incessant actions, since the Bonaparte expedition, in the hope of controlling this highly strategic region of the world. If the Western powers' policies remain unchanged, it is quite difficult to see how these cruel geopolitics can be ended, and with it the alas too often trivialized violence that continues to dig its thorny roots deeper into the history of many continents.

PART III
HOW TO ADDRESS THE COMPLEXITY OF THE MIDDLE EAST

9

WRITING THE HISTORY OF THE MIDDLE EAST: METHODOLOGICAL DIFFICULTIES

Over the previous pages, we have tried to retrace the history of the Middle East in the full scale of its length and its complexity. This task was particularly challenging as our knowledge of the Ancient Orient only developed over the course of the two last centuries through the work of numerous European archaeologists, which revealed the importance of the Egyptian, Sumero-Babylonian, Assyrian, and Anatolian civilizations. Thanks to such archaeological finds, the history of the Middle East is no longer limited to the narratives of Roman, Byzantine, and Arab historians, and it is now possible to rebuild what we have labelled the complex 'geology of cultures', which was formed like superposed sedimentary strata over the Middle East's major historical pillars, identified in the first section.

The advent of Islam in the Middle East: causes and consequences

After the rise of Christianity and later Islam, such ancient cultural sediments became buried deep in the memories of the local peoples, and new cultural layers came into sight. The advent of Islam, however, created a deep fault line between the onset of Muhammad's prophecy and the entire previous period, which was labelled the 'Age of ignorance' (*al Jahiliyah*). Islam adopted a new almanac, the Islamic era beginning with the date of Muhammad's emigration (*hijrah*) to Medina, which corresponds to the year 622 in the Gregorian calendar – the year when the Prophet was forced to leave Mecca due to the hostility of the local notables. These notables had at first chosen to remain faithful to their traditional polytheistic beliefs and strongly opposed his new message and Prophet Muhammad was forced to take refuge in Medina where he was greeted, at first, with great warmth by the vast Jewish population living there.

Muhammad's teachings, it is established and widely accepted, were largely inspired by the Old Testament and by the Gospels; they only became more elaborate when the Prophet reached the age of maturity. Hereafter, he structured his discourse as a chain of questions addressing the foremost religious disputes that had been dividing the Middle East since the advent of Christianity. Dissentions were common at that time, not only between Jews and Christians, but also between the various Christian Churches, which were engaged in fierce theological quarrels mainly regarding the nature of Christ (God and man) and the primacy and hierarchy of the Episcopal Sees (Jerusalem, Antioch, Alexandria, Constantinople, and Rome).

Such inextricably intertwined Christological and primacy disputes surfaced in a specific context, i.e., while the Byzantine Empire was trying to impose its own Christian Orthodoxy and to assert its political and military supremacy over the region. But the Byzantine ambitions did not pass unopposed; rather they evoked strong reaction and resistance, which manifested in the advent of an array of conflicting theological currents: Monophysitism (belief in Christ having only one nature, this being purely divine) prevailed in Egypt, but also found followers among the Armenians, Ethiopians, and Jacobites of Syria; Nestorianism (belief in Christ having two natures, human and divine) prevailed in Mesopotamia and Iran; and Donatism in North Africa. Arianism, which also long divided the Christian

Orient, was also widespread in various doctrines deemed heretical in Europe. During the first centuries of the Christian era, such theological quarrels often descended into widespread upheaval and bloodshed between the rival theological factions and churches.

As a result, the new Prophet endeavoured to introduce a formula that would satisfy both Jews and Christians from all theological branches. Islam, as depicted in the Koranic text, appears as a rigorously monotheistic religion quite similar to Judaism (God is Eternal, Unborn, Immortal; He transcends the world); but Christ is acknowledged as a prophet with a special status (Spirit of God), and Mary, occupying an esteemed position in the House of Islam, is acknowledged as a sacred virgin who gave birth to Jesus, while Ibrahim (Abraham) is regarded by the Qur'an as the spiritual father of all believers having cast off the shadows of polytheism to worship a single God.

Not surprisingly, Islamic teachings grew highly popular among the Aramaean populations of the region (and the Berber peoples of North Africa, albeit to a much lesser extent) during the Arab conquest, as we saw in the previous section. These peoples did not regard the Arabs as foreign conquerors coming to impose a new religion by subjugating the Middle East and the Byzantine realms of North Africa. The Arabs were seen as cousins by blood and language due to the striking similarities between Arabic, Aramaic, and Hebrew, but also because Islam's simplified dogma settled much of the acute and intricate theological disputes that existed at that time. Consequently, the Arab conquerors freed the whole region from the burden of Byzantine trusteeship.

The new Islamic culture, just as its Christian predecessor had done, eradicated the pagan culture and heritage from the region. And yet, the Syriac and Greek cultures did survive in educated circles under both Arab caliphates, Umayyad and Abbasid; the Muslim philosophers (Avicenna and Averroës, in particular) largely drew on Greek philosophy and their works were greatly appreciated in Europe in the Middle Ages. In subsequent years, however, the significance of Islamic culture shrivelled up in the Middle East (as we saw previously) with successive waves of foreign invasions impinging on the region, namely those of the Crusaders, and later the Turks and the Mongols.

For a long time Europe's phobia of Islam, to which we shall return, was mainly directed against the Turks, for the Turkish army long incarnated an ominous threat to Europe. It is often forgotten in our day, but the Turkish legacy was a major pillar of development for several vast regions in the Middle East and central Asia. At its height, Islamic civilization was forged by intense cultural interpenetrations and interactions, now buried in the sands of time; Islamic culture received considerable yet equal contributions from the Arabs, Turks, and Iranians alike, as well as significant influence from the neighbouring Greco-Byzantine, Sasanid Persian, Indian, and Syro-Aramaean civilizations. Nevertheless, it is commonplace in Europe – as in the Middle East – to narrow down the geographic scope of Islamic civilization to the Turkish and Arab realms, although in reality, it also encompassed Iran, central Asia, and India with the famous and brilliant Mughal Empire. By 'developing an effective and enduring central administration [...]', the Mughal Empire 'fostered a society in which, under Muslim lead, Muslims and Hindus shared in a common political and cultural life which in important sectors they carried out in common',[20] as argued by Marshall

---

[20] Marshall G.S. Hodgson, *L'Islam dans l'histoire mondiale* (Arles: Sindbad/Actes Sud, 1998), p. 210.

G. S. Hodgson, a renowned Islamic civilization specialist and American historian. Such great complexity made it very hard for the Middle Eastern societies to rebuild their historical patrimonies at the break of the modern era.

Writing national histories, an impossible task

Writing the history of the Middle East in 'national' mode can be particularly tricky due to the lack of such a narrative tradition in the region; here, as elsewhere, the system of the nation-state was a recent artificial graft, totally alien to the local environments where cultural and historical interplay had once been intense, but became lost in the mists of time. As the history of the Middle East is significantly longer than that of Europe, historical knowledge of that part of the world remains weak and fragmentary. The regional systems of rule have survived with remarkable stability and uniformity through the ages, but their dramatically shifting geographic extensions made it impossible for any empire to effectively dominate the region for more than just a few centuries. Moreover, the Middle East's geographic traits and its demographic fluctuations deriving from the many nomadic migratory waves have persistently undermined the stability of the regional political constructions.

Thus, the history of the Middle East seems related to, even dictated to in no small measure, by the perceptible migratory patterns of its major civilizations and empires. Its socio-political structures, however, have remained virtually the same, with occasional but rare transformations brought about by the geographic and demographic changes covered in the first chapter. Under Sumerian, Persian, Arabic or Turkish rule, Mesopotamia has retained its socio-political features: the beliefs and theologies that legitimized the various rules and rulers only changed in appearance, not in structure. This is also true of the cities in northern Syria and the Mediterranean littoral of Asia Minor: such cities have remained the high points of cultures, religion, trade, and intercultural exchange under Hittite, Assyrian, Phoenician, and Greek, and later Byzantine, Arab, Frank, and Turkish rules; they have incessantly fallen and risen anew, only to fade again in anticipation of a more favourable fortune.

Dynasties in Europe could remain sheltered and confined to narrow and remote stretches of land protected by natural borders, which in turn allowed them to progressively appropriate specific historical domains consolidated under monarchic rule, marking the end of tribal migration and the decline of its ensuing feudal autonomies. But this proved impossible in the Middle East. From the end of the Middle Ages, England, France, and Spain were to set the example for the rest of Europe, serving as nation-state models with crystallized and mythologized histories. The Germans and the Italians, the inheritors of great empires that had crumbled into competing principalities which remained in rivalry for many centuries, also came to adopt this model in the 19th century, thus reducing the multiethnic and multi-confessional Habsburg monarchy to a mere relic of the past which would crumble by the early 20th century. The Ottoman Empire and imperial Russia also met similar sad ends. In consequence, the study of history became limited to the histories of 'nations' on the European political models, whether monarchic or republican.

This is precisely why writing the history of the Middle East, whether one adopts the European or the Middle Eastern approach, can be a particularly delicate task, as European colonialism completely altered the region's millennial socio-political structures; furthermore, even the archaeological evidence of the Middle East's glorious past was a scientific product of the European invader. As a result, the fragmented states of the region find it hard to integrate this newly discovered patrimony which, apart from the Pharaonic civilization which was exclusively confined to Egypt, cannot be readily accredited to one of the new states, nor be exclusively appropriated by one of them. Indeed, how is it possible to delimit Babylonian, Assyrian, and Aramaean heritage between Syria and Iraq? What about the glories of the Achaemenids, the Parthians, and the Sasanians between Iraq and Iran? The same goes for the Phoenicians in Lebanon, Syria, and Palestine. Finally, which state can claim to be the inheritor of the kingdoms of Nabataea and Palmyra with their strong Arabic tincture, which we mentioned briefly in Part I?

This intricacy is most palpable in the Arab countries, apart from Egypt. It is much less complicated in modern Turkey because the country founded by Kemal Atatürk turned its back on its former possessions in the Balkans and Arab lands, as well as on the caliphate that the Ottoman Turks had held for so long, to centre itself on the Anatolian plateau. As a result, Turkey readily found historical continuity and specificity in the Hittites, the ancestors of the main Turkish tribes. Similarly, the modern Iranians inherited a prestigious monarchy and a specific language, which made it easy for them to forge an enduring historical personality. Although the Islamic Revolution (1979) no doubt altered the Iranian persona by reviving Shiite religious specificity and Iran's Islamic vocation, the Iranians have remained keenly aware of their rich and prestigious patrimony. In Egypt, the Pharaonic past is also an omnipresent historical marker, together with the specific religious patrimony (Monophysite Copt and Sunni Muslim). Despite its numerous transformations, Egyptian society has remained confined to its natural borders for millennia, which enabled it to retain a sense of cohesion and balance between the urban elites and the vast majority of peasants.

Nowhere in the rest of the Arab world, however, can one find a unique and specific history to provide the entities that stemmed from the dismembering of the Ottoman Empire with a solid base. The Umayyad Empire, seated in Damascus, was short-lived; the Abbasid Empire, seated in Baghdad, spanned longer, but Iranian and Turkish elements quickly gained power from the end of the 9th century. In the Arabian peninsula, neglected by all conquerors in the wake of Muhammad's prophecy, what is the value of the partitions carried out by the British and the multiplicity of small Bedouin dynasties and sultanates founded in this peninsula?

Each of the former Ottoman provinces that became independent states naturally sought to acquire historical legitimacy, but this proved to be an impossible enterprise given the absence of a tradition of centralized nation-states in the region, and the lack of cultural elites within each state to set the criteria of national character and to reach a consensus regarding the state's existential legitimacy. Hence the reference to Islam as an element of union and legitimacy eventually outmatched the feeling of belonging to an Arab entity (which ultimately failed to achieve global unity). Nonetheless, this religious reference remained fragile and failed to deliver a binding 'national sentiment'. The notion of Arab unity has no doubt constituted an obstacle for the non-Arab communities of the region (the Kurds and Assyrians of the Mashriq and the Berbers of the Maghrib), but the strong references to Islam also constitute a major hindrance not only for the non-Muslim communities (the Christians and Jews), but also for the other Muslim communities not belonging to the demographically prevailing Sunni branch of Islam (i.e. the various forms of Shiism, Ismailism, the Alawites of Syria, and the Druze of Lebanon, Syria, and Palestine). What is more, the instrumentation of Islam as the official creed by some authoritarian Arab regimes in both the Mashriq and the Maghrib, has only served to exacerbate populist opposition calls for the installation of a fundamentalist form of Islam, which they regard as the ultimate lever for social justice.

The influence of religion on historical narratives

All things considered, writing the history of the Middle East seems imprisoned by the systems of religious periodization, whether for Middle Eastern or European historians. Indeed, the major historical schisms became enshrined in common perception with the advent of monotheism. With Christianity, Europe adopted a calendar beginning with the birth of Christ: the concept of pagan antiquity is believed to comprise all that precedes that pivotal date; while Islam followed an almanac beginning with the Hegira (the year of the Prophet Muhammad's departure from Mecca to Medina). Nevertheless, those two ruptures are not as radical as they may seem.

In fact, monotheism never abolished the major socio-political structures of either the Middle East or those of the Romans and Greeks. After Judaism's failure to become the dominant religion and to control the local imperial structures, Christianity, and much later Islam, proved more successful in achieving this task. By abolishing the distinction between Jews and Gentiles, and *a fortiori*, between Greeks and 'Barbarians', Christianity managed to take over the imperial structures of Anatolia and to achieve Byzantine grandeur within just three centuries. Similarly, Islam easily took control of the structures of the Sasanids and Byzantium in Syria and Palestine, mainly by acknowledging the monotheistic prophecies that preceded it and by recognizing, albeit half-heartedly, the Persian Zoroastrian faith.

There was also no fundamental fracture between certain pagan theologies evolving toward the concept of a single deity and the successive apparition of the three monotheisms. Rather, it was the encounter and the interactions between classical Greek philosophy, in particular Platonism, and Oriental theological concepts that set the stage for the advent of the monotheisms. The theological constructions of the Middle East, whether Egyptian or Sumerian, were all subject to a rigid hierarchization system with a dominant divine figure, which could be easily confused with that of the sovereign. Persian theology stemming from Mazdaism developed the dual concept of good and evil, and right and wrong, which was to influence the three monotheisms; it was only many centuries later that the monotheistic theologies were finally able to establish their dogmas clearly and to shake off their too-obvious ties with the ancient pagan creeds. The enduring struggle of the ruling classes, in Islam as in Christianity, against the advent of heresies and mystic Gnosis that lasted until the consolidation of Turkish dominion in the Middle East and the Renaissance in Europe, bears witness to the survival of certain pre-monotheistic features. Indeed, the sects of heterodox Islam (Druze, Alawite, Ismaili doctrines) that continue to exist today, are the inheritors of the Middle East's Gnostic traditions and the living proof of the religious syncretism that the monotheistic religions tried so hard to erase. More recently, the Bahai sect, ruthlessly persecuted in Iran since the instatement of a religious government in 1979, has been perpetuating this tradition since the 19th century.

Religious syncretism profoundly marked the history of the civilizational cross roads that is the Middle East. Its imperial political structures would not have expanded so readily had religious syncretism not prevailed in the past. Indeed, the continuous enlargement of pantheons led to the combination of various deities worshiped by different conquered or federated cities and, in turn, to the shaping of large cosmogonies dominated by a single supreme deity (Ahura Mazda for the Persians, Marduk for the Babylonians, etc.). The monotheisms broke that pattern. Christianity, however, with its dogma of Trinity, its quarrels about the single or double natures of Christ and the relations between them, as well as its cult of saints, better succeeded in integrating the ancient religious architecture of the Middle East; this explains the success it met where Judaism had previously failed. Islam, a few centuries later, by striving to restore a strict monotheism to end the Christological quarrels that plagued the Byzantine Middle East, was soon caught up in the Shiite dispute: the key figure of Ali, the Prophet's cousin and son-in-law, and his dynasty of successive Imams (sometimes limited to seven, sometimes extended to twelve, depending on the different branches of Shiism), reintroduced a more complex theological structure. Indeed, the Shiite clergy still prevalent in Iran and now witnessing a strong revival in Lebanon no doubt draws strength from its predecessor, the Zoroastrian clergy.

Thus, the religious schisms which occurred throughout history were never abrupt, radical, or instantaneous. This is true of Judaism and Christianity, and even in the case of Islam despite its fulgurant rise and spread. In fact, through their political expansion the Arabs were only perpetuating the great traditions of the Middle East, where new conquerors always came with new religious concepts, yet never urged them by force upon the peoples of this region, which has always been characterized by its religious pluralism. Consequently, imprisoning the vast history of the Middle East in a periodization system based on religious events can only produce an artificial reconstruction; today still, this religious-bound approach inhibits writing the history of the Middle East based on more objective criteria, such as purely political events (invasions, the rise and fall of imperial structures, etc.), the influence of geographic environments, technical knowledge, trade routes, etc.

The historical narratives on the Middle East have mainly and increasingly focused on religion since the beginning of the 20th century, particularly in relation to the advent of Islam. In addition, regarding the ancient Middle East, archaeologists/historians have focused a great deal on the 'ethnic' origins of the different nomadic peoples that entered the region (the Elamites, Amorites, Aramaeans, Assyrians, Medes, Parthians, etc.). Nowadays we have at our disposal only monotonous narratives of Islamic civilization in which all cultural identity, geographically localized, of the different societies which make up the Middle East has disappeared. Although the names of cities have not changed since the Arab and later Turkish conquests, the layman cannot easily identify the pre-Islamic cities, nor fathom the connection between the old and contemporary names; today one has to refer to specialized guide books to notice that a given modern city corresponds in fact to a famous ancient city or is perhaps located nearby.

Furthermore, the Islamic prism has become so predominant that certain authors simply identify the entire region as 'Muslim'[21] when addressing geography. Even in his remarkable

---

[21] An example can be found in Xavier De Planhol, *Les Fondements géographiques de l'histoire de l'islam* (Paris: Flammarion, 1969); or André Miquel, *La Geographie humaine du monde musulman jusqu'au XIe siècle* (La Haye: Monton, 1967).

Grammaire des civilisations,[22] Fernand Braudel identifies all civilizations (Africa, Europe, the Americas, the Indies, the Far East) by their geographical location, except for the Arab, Persian, and Turkish civilizations, which are all amalgamated under the generic umbrella of 'Islam and the Islamic world'; even such an eminent historian felt compelled to employ the vague expression 'lands and seas of Islam', and simply wrote off the eminent Byzantine civilization, to name but one.

This very striking occurrence deserves a study in itself. Indeed, such an approach leads to the dangerous exoticization of the Middle East in the eyes of Europeans. By reducing the region to a supposedly unchanging and solidified Islamic civilization, the intense linguistic, geographic, and religious diversity which has characterized the region from remote antiquity until the present day, even within so-called Muslim societies, is denied. Incidentally, this approach objectively coincides with the vision of the Islamic fundamentalists: always ready to denounce the 'Orientalists' when their respective theories are incompatible, yet just as ready to quote them – abundantly – when it comes to asserting Islam's 'global nature' as a political and civilizational system.

The necessary rehabilitation of secular historical criteria

It is to avoid such traps inherent to historical narratives that we chose not to consider Islam as the sole element of identification of the Middle Eastern peoples, the only civilizational marker, or the unique key to fathom the events that have been tearing the region to shreds for the past two centuries. Rather, we chose to concentrate on the geographic, linguistic, and cultural aspects that have

---

[22] Fernand Braudel, *Grammaire des civilisations* (Paris: Arthaud-Flammarion, 1987).

characterized the history of the Middle East for over six millennia. This approach allowed us to identify four constant pillars in the region: Anatolia; northern (Babylonian and Chaldean) and southern Mesopotamia; the high Iranian plateaus; and Egypt. These four geographic platforms have housed numerous great civilizational structures, whose legacy remains present in our modern societies in the survival of clannish and family-like structures, of Muslim clergies and local brands of Christianity, and of patrimonial states and governors, etc. In the case of the Ottoman Empire, Dimitri Kitsikis, a contemporary Greek historian, has brilliantly demonstrated the theory of a binational Helleno-Turkish Empire[23] based on numerous supporting facts. Some city-states were sometimes encompassed in such empires, sometimes not; these included the Phoenician cities of the Mediterranean littoral, the cities of northern Syria, as well as the small short-lived kingdoms (as compared to empires), like the kingdoms of Judea, Palmyra, Nabataea, and not least, Armenia. Imperial structures were themselves fragile: they were infiltrated by vast demographic movements that weakened them at the outset, but eventually allowed them to re-emerge at the same sites by developing new cultural, political, and theological synthesises.

The Akkadians, Assyrians, Greeks, Persians, Egyptians, Arabs, and Turks have all achieved extraordinary synthesises which laid the foundations for the Middle East's imperial structures, city-states, and small kingdoms and their remarkable architecture and culture. Thus, only an approach based on geographic criteria – as is the case with Europe, China, and the Americas – allows setting sharply defined

---

[23] Dimitri Kitsikis, *L'Empire ottoman* (Paris: PUF, 1980).

notions and benchmarks in a truly objective fashion. This offers an unbiased perspective, free from the exclusive prisms of religion (paganisms/monotheisms) or race (Aryans/Semites) – which are of hardly any interest. Hence a linguistic approach validating the geographic facts is more fruitful, as is the case with the development of knowledge about the Akkadian and Sumerian languages, something which has revealed the relationship between these two ancient languages and Arabic, Hebrew, and Aramaic (Syriac).

Despite the multiplicity of names given by the ancient historians and the Bible to the various peoples of the Mesopotamian basin and the Fertile Crescent, the unity of civilization, culture, and hence the history of the Arab Mashriq remains too clear to be denied: this major region is the heir of the great Babylonian civilizations (and their Persian contributions), of the Phoenician maritime cities, and of the Aramaic culture whose language long dominated the bulk of the Middle East and survives at present in the Syriac liturgical rituals of the numerous churches of the East. Another major entity, located halfway between the Mashriq and the Maghrib and still present to this day, is Egypt. If North Africa is irrefutably Arabo-Berber, the Mashriq is positively Arabo-Aramaean.

After having long straddled both the Mesopotamian Basin and the high Iranian plateaus, Iranian civilization has turned definitively to central Asia and the Indian continent since the Arab conquest and the advent of Islam. In fact, it is in continental Asia, Indonesia, and Malaysia, not in the Middle East, that the largest Muslim states are found today (roughly 700 million out of a billion Muslims worldwide). As for Turkish civilization, after having dominated a formidable geographic ensemble extending over three different continents, it is presently confined to merely

Anatolia even if some Turkish vestiges can still be found in central Asia.

In the present day, talking about 'Islamic civilization' as if the Abbasid caliphate or the Ottoman Empire were still alive, at least politically, is equivalent to asserting that the Holy Romano-Germanic Empire is still so very omnipresent in Europe that its entire history actually coincides with that of 'Christian civilization'. Such inaccuracy is even greater with the use of the expression 'Arabo-Islamic civilization' because this implies denying the fundamental contributions of the Persians and the Turks in the expansion of Islam. In addition, such a dangerous approximation also disregards the essential Aramaeo-Syriac contributions to Arabic language and culture, as well as those of the Berber civilization, and the history of the Arab countries of North Africa.

Adopting geographic and linguistic benchmarks is thus a cornerstone in any depiction of the Middle East. The same could be said for the necessity of reconstituting events in their strictly political, and hence profane context. This is why it is essential to draw a clear distinction between the different types of history adopted to describe the Middle East; the history of religions (with its passions and prejudices) can, by no means, be a substitute for the history of the royal/imperial dynasties, or for that of the geographic regions and the peoples (with their linguistic and cultural specificities).

10
THE CAUSES BEHIND THE DECADENCE OF MIDDLE EASTERN CIVILIZATIONS

Anthropological or historical causes?

There is an enduring intellectual tradition in Europe that blames the decline of the civilizations of the Orient on the 'Semitic' character of its populations (Renan and Gobineau) or on Islam, ethnically incarnated sometimes by the Arabs, sometimes by the Turks. Eminent historian René Grousset even ventures to suggest that the whole region, since antiquity, was characterized by the struggle between the West, the heir of Hellenic culture, and the Asiatic East. He regards Islam as the 'grand revolt of Asia', manifesting in the 'Arab tide' during the invasions of the 7th century. These invasions supposedly caused an 'abrupt' recoiling of the frontiers of Europe and the Hellenic domain which had hitherto engulfed Egypt and the Syro-Mesopotamian ensemble.[24]

Marxist analysis has often illustrated its theory of Asiatic despotism with the Middle East's ancient empires or with more recent examples such as the Ottoman Empire. Despotism, religious fanaticism, the 'limitations' of the Semitic mind, and the images of predatory Arab Bedouins are all persisting themes, subliminally but more often

---

[24] See René Grousset, *L'empire du Levant, Histoire de la question d'Orient*, (Paris: Payot, 1946), pp. 7-8. Additional reading, with a much more virulent approach, can be found in the pamphlet of Jaques Ellul, *Islam et judéo-christianisme* (Paris: PUF, 2004), where the philosopher tries at all cost to show that the Muslim religion has no relation whatsoever with monotheism, exclusively incarnated according to him in Judeo-Christianity. He goes to further warn that any attempt of reconciliation with Islam would not only threaten the personality of the West, but also its security.

overtly, in the European perception of societies in the Middle East. Such images are sometimes contradicted by the works of some Orientalists who were fascinated by Islam (Louis Massignon, Louis Gardet) or more rarely by the Arabs (Gustave Le Bon). In France, some even went as far as converting to Islam (Vincent Monteil, Roger Garaudy). More recently, the new French generation of Islamologists (Gilles Kepel, Bruno Étienne, Olivier Carré, François Burgat, Olivier Roy) have even considered the political activism of the Islamist movements to be the only possible way for Middle Eastern societies to develop and modernize, especially after what they see as the failure of all the attempted European modernizing experiences, whether secular, democratic, or Marxist.

The contrast is indeed striking, as we saw at the beginning of Part II, between the Middle East as depicted by the great archaeological finds and the histories of the successive empires until the brilliant Abbasid Caliphate, and the images of sweeping economic and cultural underdevelopment we see today. Some historians blame it on the climactic changes that supposedly eradicated the material bases of Middle Eastern civilizations; but this hypothesis has been refuted by most specialists, since the barren vastness of the deserts and the rarity of rain has typified the Middle East since its earliest recorded history. Nevertheless, man's efforts to reduce the negative effects of this difficult climate appear to have tailed away many centuries ago, in particular after the demise of the Abbasid Empire and the tumult provoked by the Crusades, followed by the Mongol invasions which destroyed the infrastructure of all the cities of high culture like Baghdad, Damascus, and Tripoli. The demographic decline which beset the Middle East between the 13th and 19th centuries, which was naturally coupled with economic decline, without doubt led to the abandonment of the continuous efforts to deal with such a hostile environment. Furthermore, the reign of the Ottomans, which followed centuries of turmoil and religious warring, contributed to the solidification of religious dogma and thought, halting the creative momentum that had hitherto characterized Islamic culture. Thereafter, the torch of innovation and civilization was passed on to Europe.

After contact with the Atlantic world and the Far East through the development of navigation techniques and long-distance commerce, Europe stole away one of the Middle East's pillars of material prosperity: its vocation as a commercial junction between the three continents of Europe, Asia, and Africa. Slowly but surely, the Middle East suffocated economically as Europe, at its peak of cultural and military power, steadily developed its techniques of transport. From the 18th century onwards, the Ottoman Empire not only lost its naval control over the Mediterranean and the Indian Ocean, but also its Asiatic territorial possessions which progressively fell into the hands of Russia. The Anatolian and Mesopotamian ensembles inevitably fell into decadence after the loss of their role as a commercial crossroads, a role that they had hitherto been able to maintain. Even Islamic civilization abandoned the Middle East and moved to the Indies where it witnessed an exceptional flowering under the Empire of the Great Mughals.

The Europeans who visited the East between the 18th century and the end of the 20th century described the rigid and destitute societies they saw there. They were all stricken by the contrast between the grandeur of the ancient civilizations (still visible in the pyramids, the Greek, Roman and Persian monuments, the beautiful mosques of the golden age of Islamic empires, the Frankish ruins, etc...) and the poverty, misery, and destitution of the rural and urban populations. Europe thus decided to resuscitate the Orient via colonization. In his *Esquisse d'un tableau historique des progrès de l'esprit humain* (1795), Condorcet establishes the philosophical foundations of this design: 'These immense countries will afford ample scope for the gratification of this passion. In one place will be found a numerous people, who, to arrive at civilization, appear only to wait till we shall supply them with the means; and, who, treated as brothers by Europeans, would instantly become their friends and disciples. It is here that we will see nations crouching under the yoke of sacred despots or stupid conquerors, and who, for so many ages, have looked for some friendly hand to deliver them.'[25]

Bonaparte's expedition to the Orient in 1798 was indeed the shock that the slumbering and decadent Middle East desperately needed, although it failed to pull it from the clutches of economic and cultural underdevelopment. Two centuries later, the region is still prey to political convulsions and economical underdevelopment. The aftermath of European and later American hegemony cannot be easily defined, and we can only hazard a guess at this stage as to what will come next. In order to do so, we would like to stress once more the need to draw a clear distinction between the historical causes of this decadence, which can be more or less defined objectively, and the anthropological causes, upon which European thought insists when trying to explain its own superiority and the subservience of other civilizations.

---

[25] Quoted by Henri Laurens, *Le Royaume impossible. La France et la genèse du monde Arabe* (Paris: Armand Colin, 1990).

Western influence: a catalyst for renaissance or for more decadence?

Western infiltration into the Middle East has no doubt served as a powerful lever for multidimensional change. Indeed, this infiltration began much earlier than the Napoleonic expedition as evidenced by the intense cultural and political interplay between Europe and the Middle East since the Renaissance.

The wind of reforms in the 19th century

The Balkan and the Greek worlds were the first to be engulfed by the Ottoman Empire and thus acted as important links between Europe and the Middle East. Many high-ranking military (the janissaries) and civil (imperial architects, province governors, diplomatic officials) figures of the Ottoman Empire came originally from the Balkans (particularly Albanians, Bosnians, Romanian Greeks, as well as many Armenians). It must not be forgotten that the organization of the Ottoman Empire had once aroused the admiration of the Europeans, whose states were still embroiled in unremitting wars, let alone the ravages of religious wars. [26]

The second source of European influence was the development of Levantine colonies. These were colonies of Europeans of diverse nationalities living in the great cities of the Ottoman Empire and benefiting from the protection of the European consuls via the many 'capitulation' treaties signed between the European states and the Empire. The first such treaty was signed in 1536 by Francis I of France

---

[26] Lucette Valensi, *Venise et la sublime porte* (Paris: Hachette, 1987).-

and Süleyman the Magnificent, and was followed by several others, all granting the same privileges to other European powers. Some Levantines were probably the descendants of crusaders who had remained in the Levant after the disappearance of the Latin states, as we saw earlier. They generally served as commercial agents for the European states, but as of the 19ᵗʰ century, they started to engage in industrial activities and occasionally managed to become landowners. Another source of influence was that of the European missionaries whose numbers increased with Europe's growing conscience of the importance of the Eastern Churches. The purpose of such missions was to bring back the schismatic Christianities to Catholicism and to Latinize their liturgies.

Britain soon realized the magnitude of the political danger incarnated by the French and Italian missionaries in the Ottoman world. From the start of the 19ᵗʰ century, the British tried to compensate for lost time and American protestant missionaries were called to the rescue a few decades later. In 1862, they founded the first important English-speaking school of the region in Beirut. It became a prominent intellectual centre in the 20ᵗʰ century, and is still active today in the form of an American university. In the opposite direction, we must mention the spectacular overture of the Druze emirs of Lebanon in the late 16ᵗʰ and early 17ᵗʰ centuries to the dukes of Tuscany as part of their emancipation from the Ottoman Empire. This overture gave the Maronite community exposure to Europe; many Maronite scientists were sent to France to help in the development of linguistics (Syriac and Arabic). In 1584, the Maronite Church founded a college in Rome to which it sent its best elements to familiarize themselves with the functioning of the Catholic Church, thus unearthing dormant ties of allegiance after many centuries of interruption.

Thanks to the creation of modern schools and the printing of religious books, the activities of the missionaries produced a cultural rise among the Christian communities, especially in Syria, Palestine, and Lebanon, the privileged locations of the missionaries. But this also led to interior schisms in these communities with the emergence of groups that abandoned the traditional authority of the local patriarchs and linked themselves directly to Rome or to the different Protestant Churches. Furthermore, the carrying out of educational activities in the European way targeting Arab Christians engendered a sentiment of distancing and social alienation between the Christian and Muslim communities.

Nevertheless, European ideas also influenced a large part of the Muslim elite. At the dawn of the 19th century, Turks, Persians, and Arabs travelled to Europe and witnessed the tremendous technical and cultural progress of the great European countries, the emancipation of women, the existence of parliaments that limited the absolutism of the sovereigns, and the development of nationalist cohesions and ideologies. Modernity exercised an irresistible appeal on the different Middle Eastern elites, starting in Egypt under Muhammad Ali, and later in the court of Istanbul, and finally in Persia. Nuclei of urban bourgeoisies with European lifestyles began to emerge in major cities; the first newspapers started appearing and forming opinion in the upper layers of the urban elites who realized with deep bitterness the backwardness of the East compared with Europe and the colonial ambitions of the European states. The awakening of intellectual life after contact with Europe also gave birth to a great movement of Arab intellectual and linguistic renaissance (called the period of the *Nahda*) mainly in Cairo, Damascus, Aleppo, and Beirut. At the same time, numerous Arab thinkers in Syria, Lebanon, and Egypt, called for a reform of the Islamic morals and exegesis that had remained stagnant for many centuries, and for a limitation of the arbitrary political rule of the Ottoman sultans.[27]

A wind of reform also began to blow through the court of Istanbul. This movement came to fruition at the end of the century, following several political and administrative reforms (the *Tanzimat* of 1839 and 1856), in the forming of secret societies of young officers (the Young Turks) committed to accelerating the modernization of the Empire in order to prevent its disintegration; in 1876, a constitution was urged on the Ottoman sultan. Much the same happened in Persia where, in 1906, the monarchy was compelled to accept a constitution limiting the absolutism of the shah. Thus after several centuries of idleness and decadence, the East finally showed signs of vigour.

Adverse reactions to Western domination

Yet European influence proved corrosive as well. The immediate adverse reactions were felt on the economic level: European products, especially textiles, caused the ruin of entire sectors of the local traditional crafts and silkworm culture; the social structures of the entire region were severely affected, especially as the reforms of landholding systems and agriculture structures brought other sweeping changes in terms of land tenure and systems of exploitation. Then, on the political level, the incursions of the European states into the internal affairs of Egypt, the court of the sultan in Istanbul, Persia, and the Christian communities

---

[27] Regarding this movement, see the classic and much documented work of Albert Hourani, *Arabic Thought in the Liberal Age. 1798–1939* (London: Oxford University Press, 1967).

(Arabs in the Fertile Crescent, Greeks and Armenians in the Ottoman Sultanate, and Copts in Egypt) grew apace. And finally, on the military level, Russian pressures reached unparalleled heights in the Middle East, much like those of the Austro-Hungarian Empire in the Balkans. As was previously mentioned (see Chapter 5), in their struggle for control of the Middle East, the French and the British drove the Maronites and the Druzes in Lebanon into a deadly cycle of violence between 1840 and 1860. Beirut was bombarded by British fleets in 1840 to repel Egyptian troops; and in 1882, Egypt, unable to repay its accumulated debts towards the European financial markets and overwhelmed by the outburst of nationalism, fell under British occupation.

Such European behaviour triggered a two-fold reaction. This was first manifested in the rejection of European modernist ideas among various Middle Eastern milieus, irritated by this European penetration. Therefore, next to the voices calling for a reform of Islamic jurisprudences and institutions, other voices asserted themselves very early on as callers for a fundamentalist renaissance refusing any borrowing of ideas from Europe. The most extreme form of such fundamentalism was incarnated by Wahhabism. Wahhabism was born in the heart of the Arabian peninsula in the 18th century. It gained considerable ground toward the end of the 19th century and became the dominant doctrine of the Saudi state founded in 1925. This fundamentalist ideology advocates the reinforcement of Islamic solidarity to fight European and Christian domination; it refuses the advent of local secular nationalisms in the Middle East favoured by the dissemination of European ideas.

The other reaction to the infiltration of European views and to the hegemony of the European powers was indeed translated into the development of nationalistic ideas. This disrupted the millennial feeling of belonging to large imperial structures. Among the Arab populations, the linguistic renaissance and the attempts at religious reform led them to question the attribution of the caliphate to the Turks and to reclaim the practice of national and cultural rights; in Egypt, the struggle against the British brought an increased awareness of the national stakes among the local masses. The same phenomenon occurred with the Armenians and the Persians. Similarly, the young Ottoman officers who were striving to modernize the structures of the Empire soon realized the magnitude of the centrifugal tendencies threatening Ottoman power, and a sentiment of belonging to a common nation arose among the entire Turkish population (Pan-Turanianism).

The alternative to the rise of nationalist sentiments was Pan-Islamism, an ideology encouraged by the Ottoman sultan to counter European colonial pressures. This movement sought to create an Islamic national sentiment that would transcend the particularities of the different ethnic and linguistic groups of the Middle East, and to thwart European designs. Many thinkers, some secular and even agnostic, such as Jamal al-Din al-Afghani and Shakib Arslan, have readily joined this movement. At that time, Pan-Islamism was impregnated with the ideas of the Renaissance and did not forbid interaction between European modernity and the cultural legacy of Islamic civilization. Yet in fact, this movement bore no resemblance whatsoever to the ones that developed a century later in the form of radical Islamic movements, namely the Takfirists and the Jihadists, refusing Western culture and modernity en masse and seeking a return to the strict moralities of the first decades of Islam as reported by tradition.

Another important factor – of enduring significance in the Middle East – was the emergence of the first Jewish settlements in Palestine. This was an initiative of the Zionist movement created in Europe in 1897 under the direction of Theodor Herzl. Zionism developed in the Jewish milieus of Vienna and Central Europe, where anti-Semitism was being intensified by the rise of nationalistic ideas, but the movement truly gained momentum after the 'Balfour Declaration' in 1917. The idea was not recent; French and British diplomats had mooted the return of Jews to Palestine much earlier but the idea had received little support among the Jewish European communities, as the values conveyed by the French Revolution had allowed them to achieve legal emancipation and to acquire full citizenship. However, given the resurgence of anti-Semitism at the close of the 19th century, not only in Central Europe and Russia, but also in the European states (as evidenced by the Dreyfus case in France), and due to the perception of the Middle East from a religious viewpoint, the return of the European Jews to Palestine appeared to Europe as the most adequate solution amid the escalation of anti-Semitism. In the 20th century, the rise of Nazism and the elimination of a large part of the European Jewish communities by the German army brought a new urgency to the re-judaization of Palestine. Arab protests and the misfortunes of the Palestinians did not mean much to the Europeans in comparison with Jewish sufferings and the Holocaust.

Middle Eastern terrorism and the vision of a war of civilizations

Thus an additional misunderstanding was born because, on the Arab side, it was impossible to legitimate Europe's compensation to the European Jews at the expense of the Palestinians with persecutions in which the Arabs had not taken part. It proved difficult for both parties to realize the stakes of such dramatic and complex situations, and to assess their respective repercussions on two very different historical domains. On the one hand, the domain of anti-Semitic Europe in the case of the Zionist movement which claimed and conquered Palestine, with European and later American support; and on the other, the domain of the Middle East, where religious pluralism was a millennia-old feature and where the Arabs saw in the thrust of European Zionism yet another manifestation of Europe's blatant and frequent colonial aggressions. The rise of Islamic fundamentalist movements in the midst of the Cold War, then their conversion to violent movements hostile to Western hegemony, completed dramatizing the Arab–Israeli conflict. While these movements had previously proved to be highly efficient tools against communism in the Middle East, their permanence and their increasingly active involvement in the political life of the region – pacific for the moderate, violent for the others – brought about, imperceptibly but surely, a clear cut disconnection between a Europe that began to consider itself 'Judeo-Christian' through its Israeli extension in Palestine, and a Middle East that became an 'Islamic' nebula.

Since the 1990s, U.S. foreign policy in the region has been structured and developed based on this largely imaginary separation as previously mentioned, which only further aggravated the suffering of the Middle East. Then in 2001, the 9/11 attacks contributed to forge a new American doctrine which was quickly imposed on the entire world: that of a single threat to humanity, incarnated by a transnational Islamic terrorism likely to secure weapons of mass destruction and to threaten democracies worldwide. According to this perception, which was backed by several United Nations official documents, the purpose of such Islamic groups was to re-establish a caliphate in order to conquer the world. In many of his speeches, President George W. Bush even referred to the danger of a so-called 'Islamo-fascism', supposedly no less alarming than the old forms of totalitarianism, namely the Nazis and the Soviets. The works of renowned Orientalist Bernard Lewis, in addition to the famous thesis of Samuel Huntington, amongst others, contributed to popularize this idea of a fundamental antagonism between the Arab and Islamic world and the Western world, which reinforced the powerful psychological fault line that Islamophobia feeds upon.

On the other side of this fault line, there was a deeply bitter Arab world – bitter first because of the suffering of the Palestinians, still under occupation, and then more deeply so after the two 'Gulf Wars', which stirred vehement resentment in Arab and Iranian opinion. The misfortunes of the Iraqi people since 1991 were perceived as new evidence of the arrogance of the United States and its European allies due to their policies in Iraq and even in Afghanistan. Indeed, even though Saddam Hussein had never been very popular in the Middle East, the military power and the economic and scientific development achieved by Iraq under the iron hand of the Iraqi dictator were considered by many Arabs as assets against the military might of Israel and America's hegemonic ambitions in the region.

The brutality of the Western intervention to force Iraq into abiding by 'International Law' after its occupation of Kuwait and the hail of United Nations resolutions legitimating this intervention, eventually turned Arab opinion against the West; a West deemed too lax in implementing the law each time Israel was involved in brutal military actions in Palestine or Lebanon. The non-existence of the alleged weapons of mass destruction in Iraq, the pretext used to legitimate the invasion of 2003, succeeded in giving the peoples of the region the feeling that the Western powers had indeed returned to their old colonial demons with the aim of appropriating their oil wealth.

The economic and social question

The aftermath of European and later American influences is no less mitigated at the economic level than at the cultural and political levels. As previously mentioned, modernization brought about numerous social upheavals in nearly all the Middle Eastern realms of the Ottoman and Persian empires (the establishment of land cadastres consolidating large land ownerships, the development of irrigation networks, the introduction of cotton culture, and the decline of local crafts). To carry out their vast infrastructure and modernization reforms in the 19th century, the Middle Eastern states needed funding. They borrowed from the financial markets in London and Paris and offered European companies very generous concessions in exchange (tobacco, water, electricity, ports, telegraph, etc...). This period of modernization also witnessed a great deal of squandering and stock market speculation – very well documented by certain experts in economic history.[28] Yet, the European intentions were often commendable. In the tradition of Condorcet, these areas had to be brought back to their old glory days. Thus, Egypt became the chosen location of the French Saint-Simonians who came to the Orient in the hope

---

[28] Check Jean Ducruet, *Les Capitaux européens au Proche-Orient* (Paris: PUF, 1974); and David S. Landes, *Bankers and Pashas. International Finance and Economic Imperialism in Egypt* (Cambridge: Harvard University Press, 1958).

of fulfilling their industrialist dreams; they were the ones who engineered the opening of the Suez Canal to link the Mediterranean to the Red Sea.

Hindered economic growth

Such policies of economic modernization plunged the Middle Eastern states into crippling commercial and industrial debt and made them dependent on the European states. In Persia, Istanbul, Egypt, and Lebanon, the development of the local bourgeoisies was halted by the steadily mounting influx of European businessmen and technicians who came to monopolize the new modern economic activities. Local efforts in terms of education and literacy remained meagre and fell short of needs, especially in rural areas. Only the urban elites had access to modern education in missionary schools, and on the odd occasion, in certain public schools – lagging far behind the progress in terms of education and industrial training achieved by Japan in the same period. The elites were polarized by the linguistic and religious quarrels between the 'Ancients' and the 'Moderns' – reminiscent of the quarrels between the 'Slavophiles' and the 'Westerners' in Russia throughout the 19th century. They were also torn by contradictory allegiances: fundamentalist Islamism to counter foreign domination, loyalty to the Ottoman Empire, or modern nationalism (Turk, Persian, Egyptian, Pan-Syrian, Armenian, Kurd, Lebanese Christian, etc.).

Such intellectual concerns left no room for addressing the question of industrial mastery. European domination was first felt on the political and military levels, thus, in the 20th century, the struggle became, first and foremost, a struggle for political emancipation, in particular for the Arabs whose territories were occupied by the French and the British after World War I. On the popular level however, this struggle often manifested in the form of revolts against the European economic presence. Such was the case in Iran with the Persian upheavals of 1906 and Mosaddeq's attempt in 1950 to gain greater control over Iran's oil exploitation; and also in Lebanon, where strikes and demonstrations against the French monopolies became widespread throughout the mandate era. But such claims were most virulent in Egypt in the early 1950s. The nationalization of the Suez Canal, which served as a pretext for an Anglo–French aggression in alliance with Israel against Egypt, triggered an outburst of claims of economic independence virtually everywhere in the Third World. This was followed by a sweeping wave of nationalization directed against European interests in Egypt, Syria, and Iraq. The socialist systems established in these countries finally permitted the creation of a 'petite bourgeoisie' which, after the nationalization of foreign interests, went after those of the local landowners and upper classes. As a result, Arab foreign trade was massively shifted towards the USSR and the countries of the Socialist bloc; Arab–Soviet technical cooperation activities developed in all areas, in particular in the fields of hydraulics, the steel industry, and oil exploitation. Yet the Westerners were able to retain their economic interests in the Arabian peninsula – as well as in Iran until the fall of the Shah in 1979.

Petrodollars and Islamicization

The explosion of oil prices, first during the Arab–Israeli war in October 1973, and then during the Iranian Revolution in 1979, radically altered the economic order in the Middle East. The financial revenues derived from the energy sector were massively concentrated in the hands of Saudi Arabia and Kuwait. But the low demographic density in those two countries did not permit them to absorb such a sudden flood of revenues. The new wealth was therefore channelled towards promoting anti-communist Islamic solidarity, as we saw previously. Considerable aid and financial subsidies were distributed, but this was always conditioned both politically to obtain moderation toward the West, and economically to dismantle the centralized systems of economic management. The circulation of oil wealth also produced an impressive number of millionaires and favoured the rise of inflation due to the ensuing extensive squandering of cash and speculation activities.

Thus, the political and social structures of the region underwent yet another dramatic alteration, the second since World War II. In the Arab world, the era of the modernizing, socialist or secular petite bourgeoisie was followed by the era of the Emirs and Sheikhs, with their countless Islamic pious foundations and their Islamic financial institutions, as well as their intense religious propaganda promoting the Wahhabi brand of Islam, advocating the strictest implementation of the Shariah. The Gulf War of 1991 allowed the temporary consolidation of the hegemony of Islamic petrodollars, which had been briefly imperilled by Iraq's hegemonic ambitions. But there was also another claimant for the mantel of economic-religious leadership. The regime in Tehran also sought to export its own vision of the Islamic state by asserting itself as the protector of the 'oppressed' and the disfavoured social classes across Arab and Muslim nations. The most spectacular results of such Iranian aid were tangibly felt in Lebanon in the expansion of Hezbollah into various areas of the country.

Yet this race for Islamicization using petrodollars has inhibited the Arab world from achieving real industrialization. The concentration of oil wealth in so few hands has led to the neglect of agriculture (except in Syria), to the focus of industrial efforts on the refining and petrochemical industries to develop even further the energy sector, and to the expansion of such sectors as tourism and luxury real estate construction for the Sheikhs, Emirs and new millionaires. Lebanon had shown great industrial promise in various fields until 1974, but its economic prospects dropped considerably with the eruption of violence and warring as of 1975. Similarly, Iraq's exclusively public industry was seriously undermined by its costly war with Iran, then by the devastation brought about by the Western intervention in 1991, and finally by its occupation by the American army. The United States, faithful to its neo-liberal beliefs which it had been preaching for years, dismantled the Iraqi public sector and entirely liberalized the economy, but it failed to achieve any worthwhile or meaningful results given the chaos reigning over the country.

Iran also saw its industrial rise halted by the Islamic revolution of 1979, then by its war with Iraq. Yet, starting in the 2000s, and thanks to the third explosion of oil prices at the beginning of the century, Iranian modernization picked up the pace again.

Only Turkey witnessed a fairly considerable level of economic growth thanks to its political stability and to its privileged economic ties with the European Union, which brought about important investments to various sectors of the economy. But the Turkish economy remains financially fragile. Wealth is limited to the western part of the country, while the eastern rural areas are left on the breadline.

The negative aftermath of the oil era

· After the abrupt and durable drop in oil prices beginning in 1985, the Middle East returned, in just a few months, to being an economic lightweight. With its growing population, despite its recent slight decline, its industrial growth remained very weak, its role in international trade marginal, and its food deficits excessive, despite Turkey's surplus and Syria's well-balanced agriculture. Even after the new surge in the prices of energy resources at the beginning of the century, the economies of the Middle East remained marginal in world production and non-oil trade. In 2004, exports from the region comprising the countries of the Maghrib (counting hydrocarbon and petrochemical products) stood at just USD 520 billion, out of USD 9,000 billion in total world exports. Despite the increase in hydrocarbon prices in 2003–2004, the sum of these exports remained inferior to the amount accumulated by two small European countries, namely Belgium (USD 306 billion) and Holland (USD 318 billion).[29]

Similarly, the average GDP per capita in the Middle East (including the Maghrib countries) did not exceed USD 3,970 in 2005, against merely USD 2,170 in 2000, before the surge in oil prices. This shows the level of dependence of average income in the region on hydrocarbon prices, with nonetheless considerable disparities between the different oil-exporting countries. Indeed, in 2006, average GDP per capita reached USD 8,300 in Libya, USD 15,352 in Saudi Arabia, USD 21,395 in Bahrain, and USD 53,512 in Qatar. The levels recorded in 2006 in the countries without any oil resources revealed equally striking disparities: the poorest

---

[29] World Bank, *World Development Indicators*.

were Yemen (USD 649 per capita) and Egypt (USD 1,019), against USD 5,202 in Turkey, USD 6,028 in Lebanon, and USD 19,878 in Israel.[30]

Thus, the aftermath of the oil era was extremely negative in the Middle East, although it produced a general but very uneven increase in the levels of consumption and the standards of living. Apart from Turkey, the national economies remain extremely fragile, and, excluding hydrocarbon revenues, the industrial structures of the region do not allow the creation of sufficient jobs to meet the needs of its growing population, nor sufficient exports to balance its food deficits. The increasing levels of youth unemployment, an inevitable corollary of this situation, considerably feed the rise of Islamic fundamentalism.

At the beginning of the 21st century, most Middle Eastern economies were trapped in a rent-based economy with very low levels of productivity. Growth rates are largely dependent on oil prices and on climactic factors in agriculture-based economies lacking fluvial or ground water resources. On the other hand, in all the Arab Mediterranean countries in addition to Turkey, the amount of yearly emigrant remittances has become vital in maintaining the equilibrium of the balance of payments, but also in preventing the further decline of the standard of living of the numerous poor strata of the population.

A rent-based economy does not favour the acceleration of democratic reforms. In Europe, democracy only developed with the end of feudal privileges and agricultural rent-based economies, as well as with the rise of competitive industrial capitalism, which created numerous job opportunities, stimulated innovation, and enhanced the levels of education

---

[30] International Monetary Funds, *World Economic Outlook*.

and of basic or applied research. In the Middle East, however, in spite of the many economic reforms and structural adjustments undertaken since the 1980s under the aegis of the World Bank and the International Monetary Fund, the basic economic and social structures, even in the private sector, have remained largely determined by the rents distributed by the rulers.

Indeed, the private sector is largely dominated by an oligopolistic rule exerted by a few large families gravitating within the orbit of the rulers, whether monarchic or republican, and using their political influence to offer themselves countless privileges and immunities, including the absence of tax obligations. This is not to mention the privileges often granted to the high-ranking military hierarchies and to the bureaucratic nomenklaturas. Last but not least, the blatant or disguised corruption of the ruling classes has contributed to diminishing the modest dynamism of the modern private sector, whether in terms of investment, employment, or research and development. Under such conditions, the democratization of the countries of the Middle East seems highly unlikely, although many of them (Egypt, Syria, Iraq, and Iran) have indeed had previous experiments with democratic regimes, but this was before oil became the region's primary economic and financial resource.

Sweeping upheavals

In sum, the political, cultural, and economic results of Western domination in the Middle East were rather mixed. Western domination in such a stilted and decadent area naturally produced immense upheavals, not all negative. Certainly, the large imperial structures and the complex network of cities built on trade and crafts which underpinned them were shattered, and replaced by a multitude of states with borders sketched according to European interests. But within these new states themselves, however, this also led the rural classes of the plains and mountains to finally open up and to put an end to their millennia-old social and political exclusion and oppression by the urban elites. In many parts of the Middle East, particularly from the 1950s onwards, the rural areas underwent drastic transformations, allowing a large number of rural youths to finally gain access to all the privileges offered by the cities.

In the overall outlook of the region, the vast class of urban Persian, Turk, and Arab bourgeoisies that traditionally controlled the cultural and political power spheres saw its influence diminish in favour of new social groups of rural or Bedouin origins, that benefited from the sudden change in the major political structures and the discovery of oil in the region. Another major change was the emergence of the Bedouin states in the Arabian peninsula. Saudi Arabia, owing to its oil resources and to British and later American protection, became a leading regional power despite its demographic weakness (Saudi Arabia has a population of about 23 million inhabitants, a large percentage of which consists of transitory immigrant workers).

Fairly early on, such upheavals provoked a massive wave of emigration among the members of the formerly leading social classes to Europe, Canada, and the United States. More recently, the revolutions, wars, and blockages which inhibited economic growth in the Middle East have led to a new migratory upsurge towards Europe and the Americas. In the reverse direction, the immigration of the European and Russian Jews to the Middle East, initiated at the beginning of last century, resumed with special intensity after the collapse of the Soviet Union.

The Middle East has thus remained on the boil since the beginning of the 19th century, constantly disrupted by the numerous cultural, demographic, and political changes it has undergone. As we have seen, the patterns of change in the Middle East were dictated by the evolution of global power systems and, since the end of the Cold War, by the growing dependence on the United States. This was not the first time that this region had found itself under foreign domination in the course of its millennial history. Indeed, it was ruled by the Greeks and the Romans for many centuries, and also by the Crusaders and the Mongols (albeit more ephemerally), and was durably marked by them. Today, no one can say for sure what the Middle East will be like in the 21st century and the new millennium. This land of crossroads and synthesis may still have many surprises in store.

CONCLUSION

MIDDLE EASTERN POLITICAL SYSTEMS AND
INTERNATIONAL LAW

At the end of this depiction of the Middle East, we must raise a fundamental question which will determine the future of the region and the nature of its relations with neighbouring Europe: what kind of legal system can effectively govern this region and its insertion in the international order? There is naturally no simple answer to such a complex question; first because of the lack of legitimacy of the local political structures and second, due to the permanent foreign interferences they have been enduring for over two centuries.

As we have seen, the establishment of modern state structures throughout the Middle East's long history has remained, in no small measure, a frail reality, which by no means corresponds to the criteria that characterize them in Europe or the United States. Even though three states (Turkey, Egypt, and Iran) enjoy at least an ancient geographic base, their regimes are nonetheless constantly prey to tensions that render them fragile: Turkey still faces the Kurdish nationalist agitation, as well as growing antagonism between secular and Islamic movements, the latter empowered by the triumph of the Justice and Development Party; Egypt still endures the activities of Islamic terrorist movements, but also the electoral and social pressures exerted by political movements espousing the Islamic cause; and finally, Iran still endures strong Western pressure due to its determination to develop its production of enriched uranium and to its strong support of Palestinian and Lebanese rights to fight persistent Israeli occupation.

In the Fertile Crescent and the Arabian peninsula, all state borders, except in Lebanon, Yemen, and Oman, were defined by the colonial forces. In particular, the partition of the Mesopotamian basin between Iraq and Syria has destroyed the ancient unity of this region, without nonetheless uniting within a single entity the ancient Phoenician and Canaanite domains of the Mediterranean coast with the age-old Byzantine and Arabo-Aramaean urban settlements of the Syrian desert, scattered between Lebanon, Syria, Jordan, Palestine, and the adjacent regions of Iraq and Turkey. In Palestine, the population living in the part which has become Israeli, has undergone drastic changes with the immigration of Jewish populations from Eastern Europe, Russia, and North Africa. Today, Arab Palestinians remain without a country and find themselves entirely under Israeli occupation since 1967. Moreover, the sources of legitimacy of the Israeli state can be found in the European history of anti-Semitic persecutions, not in the Middle East. Thus it is not surprising that its existence has remained largely unaccepted by the peoples of the region, especially given that Israeli society has remained closely linked, in complex ways, to European and American societies, and that successive Israeli governments have never really tried to abolish the wall of hostility separating them from their Arab neighbours.

In the Arabian peninsula, Saudi Arabia is also a very recent state (1925), founded after a violent interior conquest and deriving its legitimacy from a strict implementation of a mythological original Islam, and a mobilization of pan-Islamic solidarity under the protective wing of the United States. This country, like its smaller neighbours (Qatar, Kuwait, and the United Arab Emirates), would never have acquired its political and financial weight without the oil riches that the Western world has been exploiting since World War II. Lastly, the wasteful lifestyle led by many royal and princely families contrasts terribly with the values of puritanical Islam that they put on show, which further undermines their fragile legitimacy.

This is why the Middle East is an ensemble in utter disarray today. Its heterogeneous components do not afford it a minimal level of stability. The military arsenals accumulated by the states of the region, including the Israeli nuclear arsenal, render the situation ever more disquieting. The various industrial blockages, in spite of Turkey's relative success, prevent this region from effectively inserting itself into international trade like the newly industrialized countries of the Far East (South Korea, Taiwan, Singapore, Thailand, and Malaysia) have succeeded in doing; and the sharp growth in unemployment levels provides the different factions of Islamic movements with fresh and ready young disenchanted volunteers every year.

The implementation of a modern democratic legal system is the only way to settle the Middle East's problems of internal and regional legitimacy regarding its state structures and its relations with the outside world. It will remain, however, unattainable for the foreseeable future unless the great European and American democracies themselves start abiding by international law, in a coherent and systematic fashion, in their relations with these countries. Unfortunately, the modern concepts of human rights, as well as the prescriptions of international law enacted by the United Nations, are only invoked, selectively and sporadically, by the democratic powers in relation to the countries of the Third World. And the banner of Human Rights is only brandished when it befits the immediate interests of these powers to exert pressure on some dictatorial regime in the Middle East pursuing regional policies deemed unfavourable to Western interests. However, those in such regimes who are traditionally aligned with the Western camp are seldom bothered even when they blatantly violate the most basic democratic principles under the guise of implementing Koranic law.

However, in the Arab–Israeli conflict as in the Iraqi and Lebanese cases, international law is manifestly implemented asymmetrically. The numerous UN resolutions calling upon Israel to evacuate the territories occupied since 1967 and those occupied in Lebanon in 1978, then in 1982, have never found a rejoinder in the international community and have never been implemented. Much the same is true of the previous resolutions regarding the right of return of the Palestinian refugees. Even the Oslo Agreement (1993) has remained a dead letter. However, Iraq was punished by the United Nations for its invasion of Kuwait with a genuinely criminal economic embargo which brought the death of tens of thousands of children and elderly, while consolidating the power of the dictator and putting in place a shameful traffic of oil exports and Iraqi imports, under the watchful eye of the United Nations. The latter, in 2003, gave their assent *a posteriori* to the invasion of Iraq by the American army and even provided it with a legal framework.

In Lebanon, the United Nations have never bothered to create a tribunal to judge the war crimes and the crimes against humanity perpetrated between 1975 and 1990 by the militia leaders and the foreign armies protecting them, nor to punish the successive invasions of Lebanese soil by the Israeli army and its totally disproportionate reprisals as was the case during the summer of 2006. But starting 2004, on the pretence of helping Lebanon disentangle itself from the Syrian web and from the presence of Hezbollah, the UN suddenly displayed a startling level of activism. As soon as the country had theoretically recovered its sovereignty in 2005 with the evacuation of Syrian troops, this newly-found independence was again mortgaged, this time to serve Western policies in the region using Lebanon, yet again, as a 'buffer state' in regional conflicts:[31] the country was thrown into the clutches of an extremely dense network of UN Security Council resolutions and declarations totally paralyzing the functioning of the state and of its judicial system. As we have seen previously (see above, chapter 8), an international investigation commission was created to identify those who were behind the assassination of Rafic Hariri, and in May 2007, a tribunal of international character was even created to try his assassins under Chapter VII of the Charter of the United Nations (authorizing the imposition of sanctions or the use of force), although after four years of existence, the investigation commission had not yet concluded its work.

Thus, democratic principles, which had raised boundless hopes among the peoples of the Middle East from the beginning of the 19th century, have become largely discredited due to the many colonial manipulations, and to the selective practice of such values by the democratic states themselves in their relations with the countries of the region. This lack of credibility has evidently been highly favourable to Islamic movements that advocate simplistic programs, often rejecting en masse the principles of political pluralism and Western-style rule of law. But even though such movements enjoy a large political and media space in the Middle East and are supported by contradictory political

---

[31] See Georges Corm, *Le Liban contemporain, Histoire et Société* (Paris: La Découverte, 2005); and also *Le Proche-Orient éclaté, op. cit.*, pp. 986–1046.

manoeuvres in Iran and Saudi Arabia, they still deeply divide public opinion in local societies. Their ostentatious practice of Islam and their claim to absolute politico-religious truth profoundly irritate large segments of the population, whether Sunnite or Shiite, not to mention the heterodox Muslim groups as well as the many Eastern Churches and their millions of followers.

This ideological battle between adherents of political liberalism and those ready to accept the authoritarian rule of religious exclusivism will remain asymmetrical so long as the democratic West continues to offer opportunistic 'state interest' justifications in its relationship with the countries of the Middle East, rather than actively promoting democratic values. Until some drastic changes are made in this respect, it is highly likely that the games of power and rivalry and the phenomena of oppression and regression they engender will continue to characterize the region, plunging it deeper into decadence. Religion will continue to serve as a convenient screen for all the lusts for power of those states with regional ambitions, drawing as they do easy and selective arguments from the extremely rich history of this area that once was the world's cradle of civilization. If modern democracy remains missing in the Middle East, none can foretell which of the long sequence of empires and kingdoms that dominated it through the ages will rise anew in the coming centuries, or what shape the region will take.

1768. –To counter Russian ambitions in Poland and Sweden, France, under Louis XV, pushes the Ottoman sultan Muhammad III to declare war against Catherine II of Russia.

1774. –Under the terms of the Treaty of Kuchuk Kainarji, Russia keeps Azov and the Crimea gains its independence, which puts it under direct Russian influence.

1798. –Napoleon Bonaparte crosses the Mediterranean and debarks in Egypt.

1826. –The onset of the reforms era (*Tanzimat*) in the Ottoman Empire.

1829. –The Treaty of Andrinople, imposed on the Ottomans by the Russian Empire, grants autonomy to Serbia and near-independence to the principalities of Moldavia and Walachia under Russian tutelage. It also acknowledges Greece as an autonomous but tributary state.

1830. –The Conference of London confirms the independence of Greece.

1831. –Muhammad Ali, Pasha of Egypt, supported by France, invades Syria, Lebanon, and Palestine; the armies of his son, Ibrahim Pasha, penetrate Anatolia and threaten Istanbul, after shattering the Ottoman troops at Konya.

1840. –Shelling of Lebanon: a coalition comprising Britain, Prussia, Austria, and Russia, formalized by the Treaty of London signed in July 1840, rushes a naval fleet to raid Lebanon and Acre in Palestine. Muhammad Ali retreats to

Egypt and abandons his expansionist ambitions. He is acknowledged Viceroy of Egypt by the European Powers.

1853–1856. –The Crimean War and the Treaty of Paris (March 1856). This treaty puts an end to the war and marks the downfall of Russia and the preponderance of France in Europe. The Black Sea is neutralized. Russia cedes a part of Bessarabia (situated at the mouth of the Danube River) to Moldavia. The Danube is opened to the shipping of all nations. To further protect Ottoman Turkey from Russia, the great powers solemnly guarantee the independence and territorial integrity of Turkey. For his part, the Sultan submits a plan of reforms to be implemented among all his subjects indiscriminately, both Christian and Muslim.

1878. –The Treaty of San Stefano (March) is imposed on Turkey by the Russian Tsar. Turkey is compelled to acknowledge Romania's independence and to cede it northern Dobrudja, in exchange for southern Bessarabia (northern strip of the Danube Delta), ceded to Moldavia earlier in 1856.

1878. –The Treaty of Berlin (July), under which Romania gives back the northern bank of the Danube River to Russia in exchange for northern Dorbrudja, taken back from the Ottoman Empire; Bulgaria receives southern Dorbrudja.

1896. –The creation of the World Zionist Organization at Basel by Viennese journalist Theodor Herzl, advocating the founding of a Jewish state.

1911. –Libya is occupied by Italy.

1916. –The Sykes-Picot Agreement between France, the United Kingdom, and imperial Russia, defining their respective spheres of influence over the Arab provinces of the Ottoman Empire.

1917. –The Agreement of Saint-Jean-de-Maurienne between France, the United Kingdom, and Italy, regarding the dismemberment of the Ottoman Empire, under which Italy is to be allotted the Turkish provinces of Antalya, Aydin, Konya, and Izmir.

1917. –The Declaration of Lord Balfour, the British foreign secretary, a correspondence in which the British government promises the 'the establishment in Palestine of a national home for the Jewish people'.

1918. –The adoption of President Wilson's 'Fourteen Points' declaring the right of the colonized peoples to self-determination.

1919. –The Paris Peace Conference is held by the victors of World War I to discuss the peace treaties between the Allies and their vanquished adversaries. Crowned by the Treaty of Versailles (June 28), it marks the fading of three empires (German, Austro-Hungarian and Ottoman) and the creation of new states in Europe.

1920. –The Treaty of Sèvres (August 10), between the Allies and Ottoman Turkey, enshrines the dismemberment of the Ottoman Empire, which is reduced to a trivial territory. The League of Nations gives France and Great Britain mandates over its Arab provinces; Italy and Greece receive some parts of Anatolia, while the treaty provides for the creation of an 'independent republic of Armenia' and of an 'autonomous Kurdistan'. After Mustapha Kemal's resounding military victories, the Treaty of Sèvres was never implemented and was instead replaced by the Treaty of Kars (1921), followed by the Treaty of Lausanne (1923), concluded with modern Turkey.

1922. –The report of the American commission of investigation (King–Crane Commission) in the Near East advocates, according to the aspirations of the local populations, the creation of an Arab kingdom unifying the Hijaz and the former Arab provinces of the Ottoman Empire. It also advises against the constitution of a Jewish state in Palestine to avoid dispossessing the Arabs and destabilizing the Near East.

1923. –The Treaty of Lausanne is signed on July 24 by Turkey on the one hand, and by France, Britain, Italy, Japan, Greece, Romania, and the Kingdom of Serbs, Croats, and Slovenes on the other. This treaty, the last of a series that concluded World War I, is obtained thanks to Mustapha Kemal's military victories. It recognizes the boundaries of the modern state of Turkey and annuls some of the provisions of the Treaty of Sèvres (such as an autonomous Turkish Kurdistan and Turkish cession of territory to Armenia).

1925. –The conquest of Mecca by Wahhabi warriors under the command of Abdel Aziz Ibn Saud; the Kingdom of Saudi Arabia is officially founded in 1932.

1947. –The United Nations Partition Plan for Palestine.

1948. –First war of Palestine; the founding of the state of Israel.

1956. –Egypt nationalizes the Suez Canal, which serves as a pretext for the Anglo–French and Israeli attack against Egypt; the attack fails after U.S. pressure.

1967. –Second Arab–Israeli war; the Israeli army occupies the rest of historic Palestine (the West Bank, Gaza, and the Arab part of Jerusalem), the Sinai (Egypt), and the Golan Heights (Syria).

1968. –Yasir Arafat, the founder of the Fatah movement of armed resistance, is nominated president of the Palestine Liberation Organization (PLO). The first Israeli strikes against Lebanon are launched (destruction of the Lebanese civilian airplane fleet at Beirut airport by Israeli commandos).

1969. –The events of 'Black September' in Jordan unfold (the Palestinian *fedayeen* are ousted from Jordan by the army and take refuge in Lebanon). The Cairo Agreement between the Lebanese government and the PLO enshrines the Palestinian armed presence in Lebanon.

1973. –Third Arab–Israeli war: the Egyptian army liberates a part of the Sinai; the Syrian army fails to recover the Golan.

1975. –On April 13, tensions in Lebanon between the Palestinian armed movements and the militia of the Phalange Party flare into open large-scale hostilities. Lebanon sinks into a civil war until 1990.

1978. –Israel invades large parts of southern Lebanon; the occupation lasts until 2000.

1978–1979. –The Camp David Agreement between Egypt and Israel leads to a separate peace settlement between those two countries. The Sinai is given back to Egypt, in exchange for American guarantees and restrictions regarding the presence of the Egyptian army in the Sinai.

1979. –The Islamic Revolution breaks out in Iran, which allows the rise to power of the religious clergy and the establishment of a new regime.

1980. –The onset of the Iraq–Iran War which lasts until 1988.

1981. –On October 6, military members of the 'Egyptian Islamic Jihad' assassinate the Egyptian president, Anwar el-Sadat.

1982. –Israel extends its occupation of Lebanon to Beirut, which is besieged and bombarded unremittingly for two and a half months. PLO fighters are compelled to evacuate Lebanon. Israeli troops do not retreat until 1985. Israel continues to occupy the same part of southern Lebanon it invaded in 1978.

1987. –Violent confrontations in Mecca (July 31) between Iranian pilgrims and Saudi police result in thousands of deaths. The first 'Intifada' begins in the West Bank and Gaza Strip (December 9). Israeli repression kills 200 people between December 1987 and May 1988.

1988. –Iraq and Iran sign a cease-fire; both countries are exhausted by war's end.

1989. –On October 22, the Taif Agreement (in Saudi Arabia) is signed by most members of the Lebanese parliament to modify the constitutional distribution of powers between the main Lebanese communities (Maronite, Sunnite, and Shiite).

1990. –Revolt of the Lebanese army commander, General Michel Aoun, who launches a war of liberation against Syria in January (his movement is aborted on October 13, 1990, after an American green light to a Syrian offensive which leads to the capture of the Baabda Presidential Palace, where General Aoun had taken refuge). On May 22, following prolonged negotiations, the unification of the two Yemeni states is proclaimed (Sanaa is the capital of the new 'Republic of Yemen'). On August 2, Iraq invades the state of Kuwait after the two countries fail to settle their financial and oil-related disputes.

1991. –The United States liberates Kuwait (January–February) with help from a large military coalition. An Arab–Israeli peace process is set in motion in Madrid.

1993. –On September 13, following secret talks in Oslo, Israel and the PLO meet in Washington and sign a 'Declaration of Principles' on interim arrangements for Palestinian autonomy.

1994. –Civil war in Yemen. Israel and Jordan sign a peace treaty. In Turkey, the Islamic party Refah triumphs in several major cities, including Istanbul, in the municipal elections.

1995. –Assassination of Israeli Prime Minister Yitzhak Rabin by a young extremist settler.

1996. –Yasir Arafat is elected president of the Palestinian Authority (January). In response to Hezbollah's strikes against Galilee, Israel launches Operation Grapes of Wrath against Lebanon (April 10).

1999. –Death of King Hussein of Jordan, his son Abdullah succeeds to the throne.

2000. –In Turkey, the Kurdistan Workers' Party (PKK) gives up armed resistance and decides to present itself as a political party. In May, the Israeli armed forces retreat from South

Lebanon, which they have been occupying since 1978, in light of the heavy tolls inflicted daily upon Israel by Hezbollah's Lebanese resistance. On June 10, Syrian president Hafiz el-Assad dies after having ruled Syria since 1970 (in July, he is succeeded by his son Bashar). On September 28, a provocative visit by Ariel Sharon, the leader of the Likud Party, to Jerusalem's Al-Aqsa Mosque unleashes widespread violence in the West Bank and Gaza Strip; the disproportionately violent Israeli response sets off a new 'Intifada'.

2001. –Ariel Sharon is elected prime minister of Israel (February). Turkey is officially recognized as a candidate for membership in the European Union (March). Syrian troops, present in Lebanon since 1976, retreat partially (they start withdrawing on June 14; on June 19, around 7,000 out of the 10,000 soldiers stationed in Beirut evacuate the capital and its suburbs). On September 11, the suicide attacks against the World Trade Center and the Pentagon kill over 3,000 people in the United States; attributed to the Islamist networks of Osama bin Laden (settled in Afghanistan), the attacks trigger heavy American reprisals: from October 7, full-scale military operations led by the U.S., with UK support, are carried out in Afghanistan.

2002. –In April, within the framework of Operation Defensive Shield (the temporary occupation of the Palestinian cities of the West Bank), Israeli Defense Forces enter the refugee camp of Jenin, killing many people. In June, Israel begins construction work on a 'security fence' along its borders with the West Bank (a barrier of 360 kilometres was to be constructed). In October, Bahrain witnesses its first parliamentary elections since 1973 (with a participation rate of over 53%, Sunni and Shia Islamists win

19 seats, independent candidates get 18, and liberals take 3). In November, parliamentary elections are held in Turkey (the moderate Islamic AKP, Justice and Development Party, wins an absolute majority with 363 out of 550 seats and more than 34% of the vote; Abdullah Gül's government, comprising only the AKP, assumes office on November 19.

2003. –Launching of the American–British-led military invasion code-named 'Operation Iraqi Freedom' (March 20). In March, the European Court of Human Rights condemns Turkey (for 'inhumane treatment' and 'unfair trial', following the arrest, detention and sentencing to death in 1999 of Kurdish leader Abdullah Ocalan, whose death penalty is later commuted to life in prison). Recep Tayyip Erdoğan is nominated as prime minister of Turkey (March); Conquest of Baghdad by U.S. forces (April); U.S. president George W. Bush announces the end of American military operations in Iraq (May); Sharm el-Sheikh Summit between George W. Bush and the Arab heads of state (June); Tripartite summit between the United States, Israel, and Palestine on the peace process in the Near East (June); In November, the American Congress imposes economic sanctions against Syria. In December, former Iraqi dictator Saddam Hussein is captured at Tikrit.

2004. –In January, Israel and Lebanese Hezbollah conduct an exchange of prisoners (under the aegis of a German mediation, Israel releases 400 Palestinians prisoners and 31 other detainees – including 23 Lebanese – and returns the remains of 60 anti-Israeli fighters, mainly Lebanese; in exchange, Hezbollah frees one Israeli hostage held since October 2000 and returns the bodies of three Israeli soldiers). In March, the Iraqi interim constitution is adopted for a transitional period from June 30, 2004 until the general elections expected to be held before December 31, 2005. In June, Paul Bremer (head of the American Governing Council in Iraq) hands over sovereignty to the Iraqi provisional government, headed by Ayad Allawi. In July, the International Court of Justice finds, in a advisory opinion, that 'the construction of the wall being built by Israel, the occupying Power, in the Occupied Palestinian Territory, including in and around East Jerusalem, and its associated régime, are contrary to international law'. (On July 20, the United Nations General Assembly adopts a resolution demanding that Israel comply with its obligations as contained in the finding by ICJ.) On September 2, the United Nations Security Council adopts Resolution 1559 aiming to free Lebanon from Syrian protectorate. On November 11, Yasir Arafat, head of the Palestinian Authority, passes away in France.

2005. –General elections are held in Iraq (January). On February 14, former Lebanese Prime Minister, Rafic al-Hariri, is assassinated. From February until April, Saudi Arabia holds its first municipal elections (the first in the history of the kingdom) – Saudis are called to elect half of the members of their municipal councils in three stages). In April, the Syrian military presence in Lebanon is brought to an end (after twenty-nine years of military presence, Syria completes the precipitated withdrawal of its remaining 14,000 soldiers from Lebanon). On June 2, Lebanese journalist and left-wing activist Samir Kassir is assassinated in Beirut. In October, the Iraqi draft constitution is approved by a national referendum (the text is adopted by 78% of the votes, with a participation rate of 63%; it is rejected by the provinces of Al-Anbar and Salahuddin by more than two-thirds of the votes). In October, Turkey's EU accession negotiations are officially launched. Lebanese MP and journalist Gebran Tueni is assassinated (December).

2006. –In January, Israeli Prime Minister Ariel Sharon is debilitated by a massive stroke which leads him to retire from political life, and power is transferred to Deputy Prime Minister Ehud Olmert. In the occupied Palestinian territories, the Islamists of Hamas sweep the elections with 76 out of a total of 132 seats in the Palestinian Legislative Council, against only 43 for Fatah (January). Ismail Haniyeh (Hamas) becomes the new Palestinian prime minister (February). Following the victory of Hamas in the legislative elections, the European Union decides to withhold a part of its aid to Palestine in April; from July 12, until August 14, tensions between Israel and Lebanese Hezbollah break out in armed conflict. On November 21, Lebanese Minister of Industry Pierre Gemayel is assassinated. The report of the American Baker-Hamilton commission advocates a change of strategy in Iraq (December). The first legislative elections in the United Arab Emirates take place (December). Former Iraqi president Saddam Hussein is executed by hanging (December).

2007. –Relations between Hamas and the Palestinian Authority greatly deteriorate. Following Saudi mediation, a government of national unity is formed under Hamas's Ismail Haniyeh. The situation on the ground, however, spirals out of control and the Gaza Strip under Hamas control secedes politically from the Palestinian Authority in the West Bank in June. This brings Israeli reprisals upon Gaza, which is submitted to an economic embargo by the Israeli army. In November, the U.S. Government convenes a peace conference in Annapolis in an attempt to accelerate an eventual settlement of the Palestinian–Israeli conflict. In

Lebanon, the wave of assassinations of political figures continues, in spite of the creation of an International Tribunal in The Hague. The authority and legitimacy of the Lebanese Government is hotly contested by the opposition after the resignation of its ministers from the cabinet; there are unsuccessful massive popular movements to bring down the Government. The terrorist group *Fatah El Islam* attacks the Lebanese army in northern Lebanon around the Palestinian refugee camp of Nahr El Bared; the fighting goes on for three months, causing the loss of many lives in the rank and file of the army. In Iraq, violence against the U.S. Army and between rival Iraqi factions continues. In Lebanon, constitutional institutions are paralyzed by the political crisis and are unable to elect a successor to President Emile Lahoud, whose mandate expired in September.

2008. –Israeli launches repeated attacks against the Gaza Strip, then in June a truce is agreed between Israel and Hamas. Egypt erects a wall on its border with Gaza and the economic blockade continues. There is a political crisis inside the Israeli cabinet, but in December–January, the Israeli army launches a dreadful attack against the Gaza Strip lasting three weeks, leaving 1300 Palestinians dead and 5000 wounded. In Lebanon, on May 7 and 8, following a decision to dismantle the communication network of Hezbollah by the hotly contested Government, Hezbollah and its allied political parties take military control of strategic locations in West Beirut before handing them to the Lebanese army. A reconciliation meeting of Lebanese leaders is held in Doha (the capital of Qatar) under the chairmanship of the Emir and agreement is reached on the election of General Michel Suleyman, commander in chief of the Lebanese army, to the Presidency of Lebanon as a successor to Emile Lahoud, and on a new government of 'national unity'. In July, an exchange of prisoners takes place between Hezbollah and Israel, despite the fact that the conflict in 2006 was due to Israel's refusal to free Lebanese prisoners held in its jails and the subsequent kidnapping of two Israeli soldiers on the border by Hezbollah fighters. Imad Maghnieh, one of Hezbollah's most important military planners, is assassinated in Damascus. There is a progressive return to normal relations between Western governments and the Syrian regime. The Mediterranean Union is launched by French President, Nicolas Sarkozy, in July in Paris. The UN Inquiry Commission tasked with finding the culprits for the assassination of Hariri and other political figures is unable to arrive at a conclusion. In Iraq, bomb attacks against Christians provoke the mass emigration of 500,000 Iraqi Christians (September–October). In December, a security treaty is signed by the United States and the Iraqi Government, providing for the future withdrawal of the U.S. army.

2009. –President Obama takes office in the United States and promotes a new political discourse towards the world and the Middle East in particular (and more specifically Iran) to improve the U.S. image after the devastating Bush years. He shows openness and understanding in his Cairo speech in June, and a will to accelerate a solution to the Palestinian–Israeli conflict and to re-establish a dialogue with Iran. The U.S. doctrine on Palestine, however, is not changed in substance, as more concessions are asked from Arab countries vis-à-vis Israel in terms of establishing normal diplomatic, political and economic relations before exerting strong pressure on the Israeli government to stop expanding settlements in the West Bank. In Israel, parliamentary elections bring the fall of the former coalition government between Kadima and the Labor Party; Benjamin Netanyahu becomes Prime Minister and continues his former policy of settlement expansion. Elections also take place in Lebanon in June under the eyes of many international observers. A spectacular mobilization of Lebanese voters, a flood of electoral money to bribe poor voters and the arrival of many thousands of Lebanese emigrants bring a majority of seats to the anti-Syrian alliance of 14th March, but not a majority of popular votes. Syria and Lebanon exchange ambassadors. After the elections, Druze leader Walid Jumblatt, a pillar of the 14th March alliance, announces that he is no longer part of it and wants to re-establish contacts with Syria. Western governments, including the United States, continue to normalize relations with Syria. In Iraq, U.S. troops are redeployed outside of the big towns, but sectarian violence continues, in addition to violence between Kurds and Arab Iraqis in northern towns (Kirkuk and Mosul). Yemen slides into domestic violence between the State and a group of dissidents.

BIBLIOGRAPHY

The first Mesopotamian civilizations

GARELLI Paul, *Le Proche-Orient asiatique*, vol. 1, *Des origines à l'invasion des peuples de la mer* (Paris: PUF, 1969). And *Le Proche-Orient asiatique*, vol. 2, *Les Empires mésopotamiens, Israël* (Paris: PUF, 1974).

KRAMER Samuel Noah, *L'Histoire commence à Sumer* (Paris: Arthaud, 1986).

MARGUERON Jean-Claude, *Les Mésopotamiens*, vol. 1, *Le Temps et l'Espace*; vol. 2, *Le Cadre de vie et la pensée* (Paris: Armand Colin, 1991).

PETIT Paul, *Précis d'histoire ancienne* (Paris: PUF, 1962).

Iran and the first Iranian empires

BANI SADR Abol Hassan, *Le Complot des ayatollahs* (Paris: La Découverte, 1989).

DIGARD Jean-Pierre, HOURCADE Bernard, RICHARD Yann, *L'Iran au XXe siècle* (Paris: Fayard, 1996).

MARTIN Vanessa, *Islam and Modernism. The Iranian Revolution of 1906* (London: I.B. Tauris, 1989).

ROUX Jean-Paul, *L'Asie centrale: histoire et civilisations*

(Paris: Fayard, 1997). And *L'Histoire de l'Iran et des Iraniens. Des origines à nos jours* (Paris: Fayard, 2006).

SHAYEGAN Daryush, *Qu'est-ce qu'une révolution religieuse?* (Paris: Albin Michel, 1991).

The Byzantine Empire, the Turks, and the Ottoman Empire

CAHEN Claude, *Orient et Occident au temps des croisades* (Paris: Aubier, 1983).

COPEAUX Étienne, *Espace et Temps de la nation turque. Analyse d'une historiographie nationaliste 1931–1993* (Paris: Éditions du CNRS, 1997).

DUCELLIER Alain, KAPLAN Michel, MARTIN Bernadette, *Le Moyen Âge en Orient*. And *Byzance et l'Islam, des Barbares aux Ottomans* (Paris: Hachette Classiques, 1990).

GROUSSET René, *L'Empire du Levant. Histoire de la question d'Orient* (Paris: Payot, 1949).

KITSIKIS Dimitri, *L'Empire ottoman* (Paris: PUF, 1991).

LANDES David, *Bankers and Pashas. International Finance and Economic Imperialism in Egypt* (Cambridge: Harvard University Press, 1958).

LEWIS Bernard, *Islam et Laïcité. La naissance de la Turquie moderne* (Paris: Fayard, 1988).

MANTRAN Robert (ed.), *Histoire de l'Empire ottoman*

(Paris: Fayard, 1989).

ROUX Jean-Paul, *Histoire des Turcs. Deux mille ans du Pacifique à la Méditerranée* (Paris: Fayard, 1984).

SHAW Stanford, *Histoire de l'Empire ottoman et de la Turquie* (Roanne: Éditions Horvath, 1983).

TATE Georges, *Les Campagnes de la Syrie du Nord du IIe au VIIe siècle* (Paris: Librairie orientaliste Paul Geuthner, 1992).

VALENSI Lucette, *Venise et la Sublime Porte* (Paris: Hachette, 1987).

VANER Semih (ed.), *La Turquie* (Paris: Fayard, 2006).

The Arabs and Egypt

BERQUE Jacques, *L'Égypte. Impérialisme et révolution* (Paris: Gallimard, 1967).

CORM Georges, *Le Proche-Orient éclaté* (Paris: Gallimard, 2007).

HITTI Philip, *History of the Arabs* (New York: Macmillan, 1972).

HOURANI Albert, *Histoire des peuples arabes* (Paris: Seuil, 1993).

LACOUTURE, Jean and Simone, *L'Égypte en mouvement* (Paris: Seuil, 1962).

LACOUTURE, Jean, *Nasser* (Paris: Seuil, 1971).

LAURENS Henri, *Le Royaume impossible. La France et la genèse du monde arabe* (Paris: Armand Colin, 1990). And *Le Grand Jeu. Orient arabe et rivalités internationales depuis 1945* (Paris: Armand Colin, 1991).

RODINSON Maxime, *Les Arabes* (Paris: PUF, 1991).

THOBIE Jacques, *Ali et les quarante voleurs. Impérialismes et Moyen-Orient de 1914 à nos jours* (Paris: Messidor/Temps actuels, 1985).

Islam

CORM Georges, *La Question religieuse au XXIe siècle. Géopolitique et crise de la postmodernité* (Paris: La Découverte, 2006). And *Orient-Occident, la fracture imaginaire* (Paris: La Découverte, 2002).

HODGSON Marshall G.S., *L'Islam dans l'histoire mondiale* (Paris: Sindbad/Actes Sud, 1998).

LAOUST Henri, *Les Schismes dans l'Islam* (Paris: Payot, 1965).

MIQUEL André, *La Géographie humaine du monde musulman* (Paris: Mouton, 1967).

PLANHOL Xavier de, *Les Fondements géographiques de l'histoire de l'Islam* (Paris: Flammarion, 1968). And *Les Nations du Prophète: manuel géographique de politique musulmane* (Paris: Fayard, 1993).

SOURDEL Dominique and Janine, *La Civilisation de l'Islam classique* (Paris: Arthaud, 1976).

Additional reading

CORM Georges, *L'Europe et l'Orient. De la balkanisation à la libanisation, histoire d'une modernité inaccomplie* (Paris: La Découverte, 2002). And *Le Liban contemporain. Histoire et société* (Paris: La Découverte, 2005).

DIECKHOFF Alain, *L'Invention d'une nation: Israël et la modernité politique* (Paris: Gallimard, 1993).

DUCRUET Jean, *Les Capitaux européens au Proche-Orient* (Paris: PUF, 1974).

LEMERCIER-QUELQUEJAY Chantal, *La Paix mongole* (Paris: Flammarion, 1970).

PIRENNE Jacques, *Les Grands Courants de l'histoire universelle* (Paris: Albin Michel/La Braconnière, 1959).

RECLUS Élisée, *Nouvelle Géographie universelle* (Paris: Librairie Hachette, 1884).

SELLIER Jean et André, *Atlas des peuples d'Orient. Moyen-Orient, Caucase, Asie centrale* (Paris: La Découverte, 1993).

SOLIMAN Lotfallah, *Pour une histoire profane de la Palestine* (Paris: La Découverte, 1989).